LONG BEACH STATE

· A Brief History ·

BARBARA KINGSLEY-WILSON | Foreword by Lee Brown

THE
History
PRESS

Published by The History Press
Charleston, SC 29403
www.historypress.net

Front cover, top left: Misty May originally played volleyball for Long Beach State. *Courtesy of Long Beach State Athletics. Top middle*: Cars parked on campus looking down toward lower campus. *Courtesy of CSULB. Top right*: Veterans Administration water tower. *Courtesy of CSULB. Bottom*: The Pyramid. *Courtesy of CSULB.*
Back cover, top: Long Beach State campus. *Courtesy of CSULB. Inset*: Students in the early 1950s show their enthusiasm for the new college going up on the outskirts of town. *Courtesy of CSULB.*

First published 2015

Manufactured in the United States

ISBN 978.1.62619.601.8

Library of Congress Control Number: 2015941003

For mom, the family historian and writer

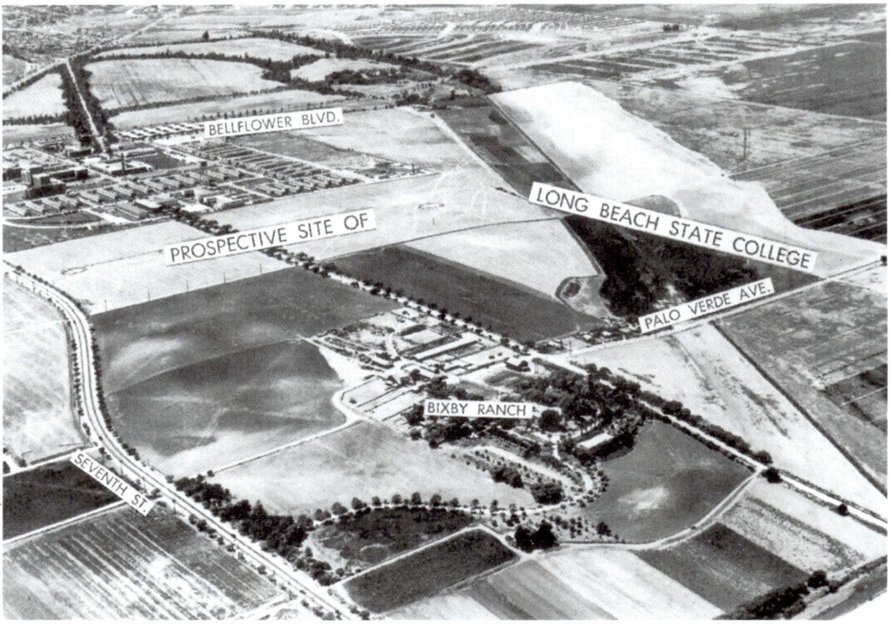

An early shot of the future campus when it was a gleam in state officials' eyes. The Veterans Administration complex is on the upper left, and streets and houses are being carved out of bean fields on the upper right. *Courtesy of CSULB.*

Contents

Foreword

For the original 169 students, attending Long Beach State College began with the typewritten schedule of classes for the fall of 1949. There were fifty-three courses offered in thirteen departments: art, biology, business, economics, education, English, geography, history, law, music, nature study, physical science, political science, psychology, sociology and speech. All of these classes were crammed into two converted apartment houses near the present campus.

Eight departments scheduled only one course that semester. Education, the largest department by far, offered fourteen courses in seventeen sections. Several of the departments also offered courses such as Art for Elementary Teachers, Children's Literature and Public School Music. All of this underscores the fact that teacher education was the primary mission of the new college.

This concise history of what is now California State University, Long Beach is enriched by the author's ability to reach back to the beginning through interviews, both recorded and first person, with the original faculty and staff and their progeny.

Barbara Kingsley-Wilson has uncovered recordings, photos and films that collectively document the early years. Moreover, she has interviewed many of the second-generation members of the campus community who contributed to its explosive growth and development.

Her background as a journalist has stood her in good stead in this effort. She not only knows how to interview, but she also knows how to gather

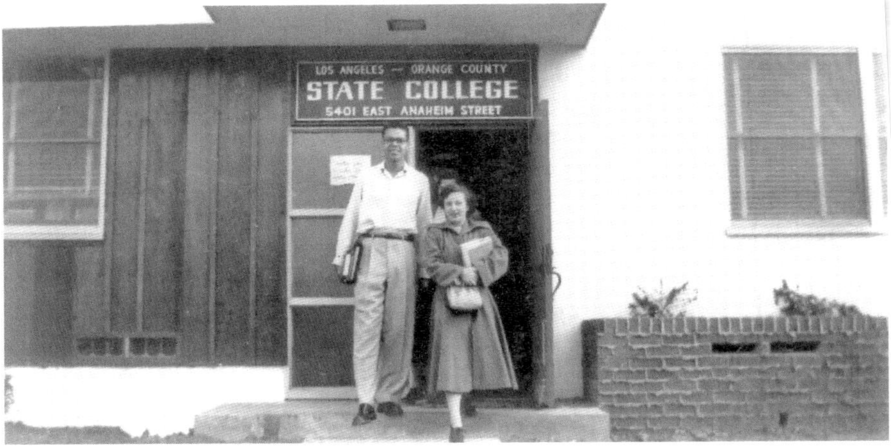

Two of the first students, Roger Bryson and Joanne St. Louis, walking out of one of the converted apartments in the fall of 1949. Bryson would become the college's first student body president. *Courtesy of the University Archives.*

information and present it in a coherent manner. More than anything else, though, Kingsley-Wilson has uncovered many of the small things—the little-known, overlooked or forgotten facts that, when integrated into the larger picture, lend texture to the fabric of institutional history.

From 1949, fast forward more than sixty years to the 2013–14 academic year, when the lushly landscaped California State University, Long Beach had about thirty thousand undergraduate and five thousand graduate students. It had become a significant university, and its students were variously pursuing about 150 bachelor's or master's degrees, as well as 5 doctoral degrees.

Those degrees were being offered through seven academic colleges: arts, education, liberal arts, engineering, health and human services, natural sciences and mathematics. Collectively, these colleges are composed of more than seventy academic departments.

By 2014, the college library, which began in 1949 with no books, had become the University Library, with holdings that included more than one million books, videos, print journals and maps, as well as seventy thousand scholarly journals, mostly electronic.

I transferred to Long Beach State in 1958. It was a time when students stood in long lines to register for courses each semester, and students often parked along East Seventh Street or in unpaved fields on north campus. Enrollment passed ten thousand in the fall of 1959, and the lines got longer.

The first two dormitories opened—one for men and one for women—but it still was (then as now) largely a commuter campus.

I was among the tens of thousands of GI Bill students who attended colleges and universities after the Korean conflict ended in 1953. I transferred to Long Beach State to study journalism, although all the journalism courses were in the English Department. I was one of the relatively few veterans who became involved in campus activities, and I was named editor of the *Forty-Niner* and elected treasurer of the Associated Students. A year after graduating and after earning an MA at the University of Iowa, I returned to Long Beach State as assistant manager of the college's news bureau, a job I held from 1961 to 1963, when I turned to newspaper work.

Nearly fifty years after my 1960 graduation, I again returned, this time as chairman of the Department of Journalism, a position I held from 1998 to 2001. After retiring, I continued as a part-time faculty member through 2014.

I often think back to my undergraduate days at Long Beach State and remember a conversation I had with my favorite English professor, Dr. Frank Nelson. I wanted reassurance that I was attending a "good" college. He replied that I was receiving a good liberal arts education and that it should take me a long way. He was right, and in my path to a doctorate—through newsrooms and university classrooms—I never had cause to look back with even a trace of regret. As I read the pages of this book, I look back with affection and gratitude.

LEE BROWN
Class of 1960

Preface

Colleges are often seen as steady, venerable institutions where change comes at a glacial pace. However, in the early days, Long Beach State was a slap-dash affair. College leaders had a month to prepare for its first semester. When students reported to classes—held in two unfinished apartment buildings—they were far outnumbered by construction workers with toolboxes and tarps.

Early students and faculty saw themselves as pioneers, and they were. Classes began on September 28, 1949, but the first book didn't arrive at the one-room wooden-shack library until a few weeks before Christmas. Sheep roamed the lower campus as late as the 1960s. Students who were forced to park in the rain and mud risked watching their cars slide downhill like Matchbox toys.

These raw beginnings gave Long Beach State a scrappiness that has continued even after buildings and trees crowded the campus and enrollment exploded.

A white-gloved woman and her feisty colleagues helped forge a sports program that launched many instructors and female sports decades before the Title IX equality laws.

One hard-charging president labeled "Robin Hood" challenged the powerful National Collegiate Athletic Association (NCAA), and his ideas helped pave the way for poorer schools like his to share in lucrative NCAA television revenues.

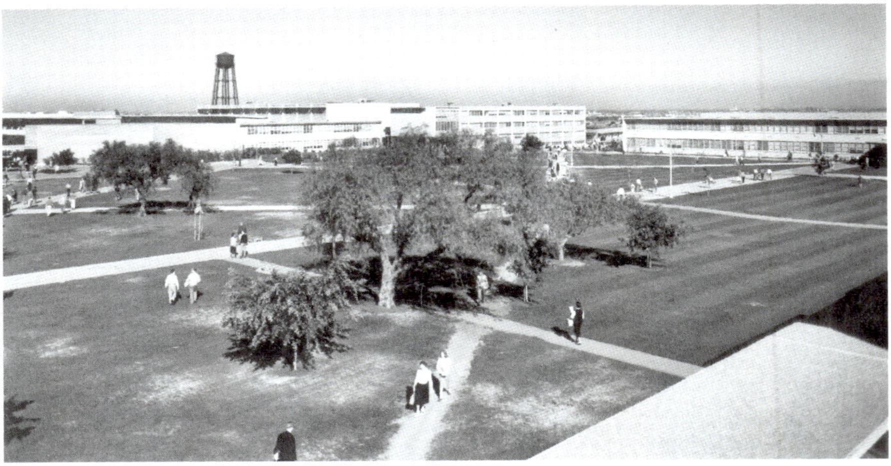

The late 1950s view from Fine Arts 1. Liberal Arts 5 and Faculty Office 3 are in the background. Some of the original pepper trees are in the center. *Courtesy of the University Archives.*

This pioneering spirit boomeranged at times, as when campus officials tried to push through a retail-and-housing complex on land inhabited one thousand years earlier by Native American tribes that considered it holy.

Yet the college pulled off another ambitious scheme, wild in its scope and size: an eighteen-story, blue-walled pyramid athletic complex that today stands as the symbol of the college.

Long Beach State, which turns sixty-six in 2015, may never be a venerable institution. But it remains scrappy, and so do its students. From the start, many have been first-generation college students, often on tight budgets, holding down one, two or three part-time jobs to pay the bills. This will always be a largely commuter campus, but it retains a strong team spirit and a track record of beating the odds.

The idea for this book came from a visit to a local Long Beach bookstore. There on the shelf was a sepia-toned history book about California State University, Dominguez Hills. I was not well acquainted with the Dominguez Hills campus twelve miles west, but I knew it was smaller and newer than the institution where I teach, Long Beach State.

You'd think, then, that there would be a similar book about the local college, which is eleven years older and larger by twenty thousand students.

I asked the folks at University Public Affairs, whom I thought would know. Nope, no book, they said. There have been mentions of the university's history in other books but to date no published work of the college history.

Before I came to work in Long Beach State's Department of Journalism and Mass Communication, I was a reporter for twenty years. Lots of journalists enjoy history, and I'm no different; my bookshelf is full of books on Long Beach history and the old Pike, even though I never set foot on the iconic seaside amusement park.

Pushing aside the notion that it's perhaps unwise to write about one's workplace (don't try it), especially while performing one's full-time job while raising a family (ditto), I convinced the people at The History Press that this would be a decent book and that I could write it.

When I queried the good folks at the university archives about what photos and records they had on hand, the head archive librarian at the time mentioned that when others had started to write a history of the university, they gave up—there was just too much there.

I can certainly understand what she meant. The life of a university has so many threads—the land, the buildings, academics, academic politics, governance, sports, campus life and alumni, just for starters. Then there are all the unpredictable events that occur at an institution largely run for the purpose of educating energetic, unpredictable twenty-somethings. There's easily enough material for twenty books.

This particular book takes what I'd call a foundational approach fans of the TV show *How the States Got Their Shapes* might recognize. There's a lot here about how things came to be—the college, some of the sports programs, campus design, the Pyramid, et cetera. There's also a short history of some of the ongoing banes of student life, such as parking.

This book uses live interviews, documents and oral histories, including oral histories from presidents P. Victor Peterson and Stephen Horn that haven't been released before.

The title, *Long Beach State: A Brief History*, came to be partly because my publisher fancies short titles. Also, mindful of the words of the university archivist, I wanted to make this a brief history. This book is not comprehensive. It tries to tell the stories of the students, faculty, staff and administrators whose labors created a college that started with 169 students and grew to 36,000 students, making it one of the three largest (along with California State University, Northridge and California State University, Fullerton) in the California State University system, the biggest university system in the country.

Preface

Journalists are fond of saying everyone has a story. (A colleague once remarked that not all of them are worth telling.) The story of Long Beach State is a story of large egos, resilience, perseverance, big ideas that worked and big ideas that didn't. Long Beach State has many good stories from its crazy, mid-century founding to the present.

I try to tell some of them here.

Acknowledgements

This is a fairly small book, but there are a lot of people to thank. I'll start with the patient Heather Steele in the university archives, who found countless photos, interview transcripts and other great materials. Robert Freligh also cheerfully provided numerous images of the old days, as did Roger Kirk of the Long Beach State Athletics Department, Janet Romain of the Marketing and Communications Department and Gay Arakawa of Alumni Relations. All were so responsive and patient with my twitchy, last-minute requests.

The Historical Society of Long Beach was also helpful in finding newspapers and photos about the founding of the college.

This book owes a big debt to David Bernstein and Kaye Briegel, whose unpublished history "California State University, Long Beach: A Historical Overview" was so helpful and thorough. Also, I'm grateful to Briegel and all the people who made the digital oral history possible. Those accessible records of the university's crazy early days, as well as the detailed summaries of conversations, were invaluable to my research as they are and will be for countless others. Tim Grobaty of the *Long Beach Press-Telegram* generously provided photos from the newspaper archives, as well as his own memories of growing up alongside the college.

Also, I'm grateful to my many patient interview subjects, but especially Jon Regnier, the former facilities director, who helped provide so much background and information on the campus physical plant. And the families of former presidents P. Victor Peterson and Stephen Horn

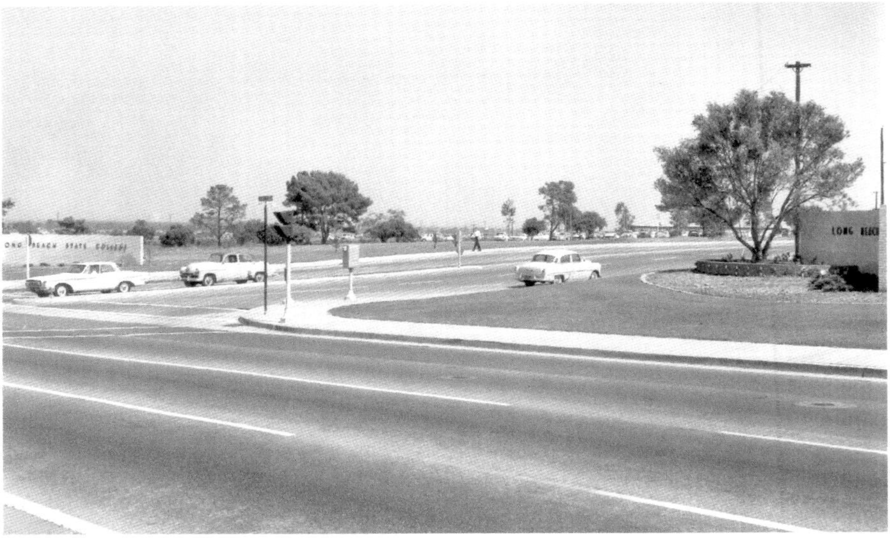

The Bellflower entrance to the campus in the early 1960s. *Courtesy of the University Archives.*

generously provided oral histories of the men who were so instrumental in developing the college.

Thanks to my wonderful writing group: Rebecca Allen, Marla Jo Fisher, Iris Yokoi, Mary Anne Perez, Robin Hinch and Lori Basheda. All offered thoughtful, concrete ideas and encouragement and really fabulous snacks. Thanks to Rabiya Hussain, who gave solid research assistance and helped tie down reporting loose ends. A shout out, too, to The History Press editors Ben Gibson and Katie Stitely, who were patient with this first-time author's many questions. Also, thanks to Jerry Roberts for getting me started on this little adventure. Editors Scott Wilson and Deborah Schoch were just mensches in the final deadline days.

Finally, thanks to my family—Scott, Ellie and Drew—for putting up with Mom as she stared at her computer for so many months. You handled this, as you do many other little challenges, with grace and a sense of humor.

Introduction

What's in a Name? Don't Ask

Picking a title for this book has almost been as hard as writing it. That's partly because this particular university has a lot of names and never quite settled on one.

The college name has changed several times since its 1949 founding:

1949: Los Angeles–Orange County State College
1950: Long Beach State College
1964: California State College at Long Beach
1968: California State College, Long Beach
1972: California State University, Long Beach

And that's just the beginning. The sports teams always use Long Beach State and always have.

Academics tend to like the longer name, as California resonates the world over. And, of course, the official name ties the university to the California State University system. Recently, there was talk of changing the name to Long Beach State to centralize the brand and conjure images of sand and sun to help draw students from California's rural enclaves.

That's the "official" name. We haven't even gotten to nicknames yet. The first students decided on the Forty-Niners (also written 49ers), a reference to the date the college was founded and the hurly-burly of the gold rush years in Northern California one hundred years before. Many years later, a popular president popularized the Beach, which is used at least as much as the original moniker.

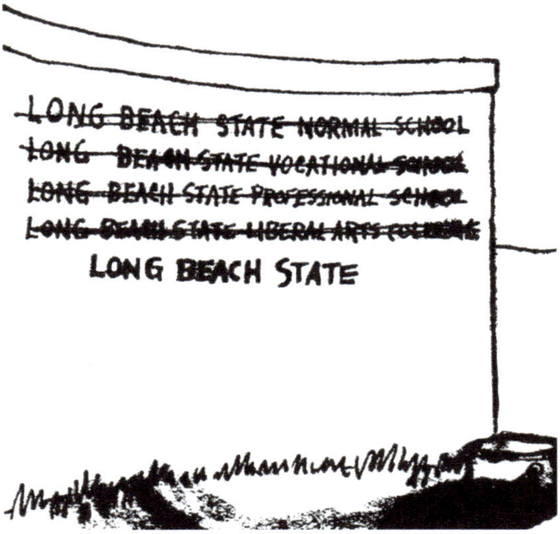

Long Beach State, or Cal State Long Beach, has many names, and many identities. *Courtesy of the* Forty-Niner.

Meanwhile, old-timers like to call the university "State," as in, "Did you see that State beat Fullerton Saturday?" That's probably an old contrast to Long Beach City College, which was "City." And many shorten the official name to Cal State Long Beach.

The local newspaper, the *Long Beach Press-Telegram*, has complained about this dual identity over the years. Editor Rich Archbold recalled asking President Stephen Horn his position on the matter in the 1970s. "Well, let me tell you something, Mr. Archbold," the editor recalled the president saying, "if Cal State Long Beach wins a Nobel Prize, we'll be CSULB. If one of the sports teams wins a national championship, you can say Long Beach State." President Jane Close Conoley also said in 2015 that the university would have at least a couple names for the forseeable future.

So pick one! It's fair to say the historic name is Long Beach State, and that's the sports name, too. This particular book spills ink on both, so that's the name that will be used on the pages here.

The hodgepodge of names is like the college's founding—a little messy and a little crazy and carried out with lots of enthusiasm.

1
No Buildings, No Books

"My God, What Have I Gotten Into?"

History professor Irving Ahlquist loved his students at Iowa State Teachers College. He was an energetic, popular professor who found all sorts of ways to engage them, including jumping up on a chair to reenact a slave auction.

He did not, however, love the winters in Cedar Falls, Iowa. He was also frustrated by the lack of housing in the city, where his family was forced to live for a time in a Quonset hut.

When Ahlquist learned that an administrator was in town to recruit professors for a brand-new California college, he jumped at the chance. Ahlquist had good memories of the Golden State from his wartime service, when he had helped escort thirty-six thousand Italian prisoners through the Long Beach harbor. Now he was eager to leave for the sun in booming California. A young man with a new family, he was ready for a new start.

As he drove through the dirt roads and lima bean fields of east Long Beach in September 1949, he was about to discover just how new that start would be. He couldn't find the campus on any maps, and no one seemed to have heard of it. When he finally did locate the college, he discovered that his new place of employment—the institution that had prompted him to move his family nearly two thousand miles—was an unfinished apartment building in a dusty, under-construction development.

"It was nothing but stacks of lumber," he said. "And I remember vividly my response to my wife: 'Why, why did we leave?'"

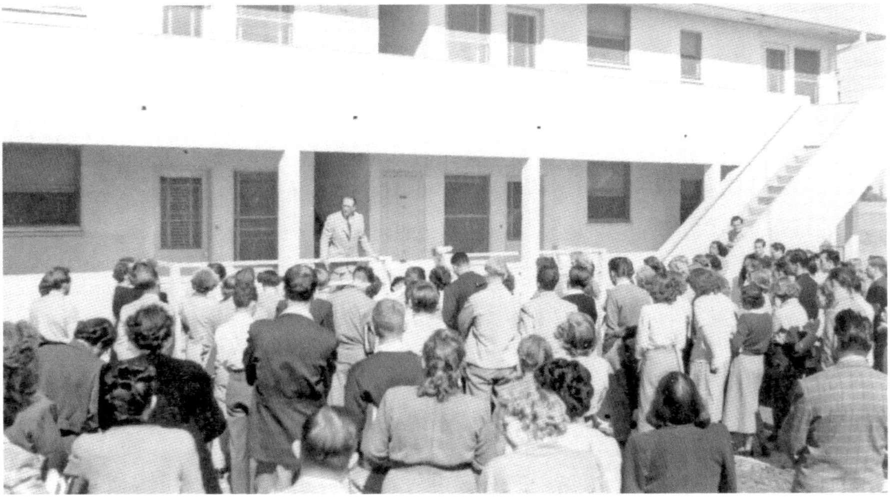

Dean of students David Bryant addresses the student body in September 1949. *Courtesy of the CSULB Archives.*

The Iowa teachers college he had left was founded before the Civil War, and he wasn't expecting ivy-covered buildings in Long Beach. "But the reality of the situation was such that it suddenly hit me. No buildings, no books, nothing."

Two years later, Professor Richard Wilde found himself on a similar trek to Long Beach from Wisconsin. Driving through the mountains in his Austin A40 with his pregnant wife, he felt grateful to have his new $4,300-a-year assignment at a time when college jobs were scarce.

Wilde was a bit puzzled that the man who interviewed him, President P. Victor Peterson, didn't seem interested in his academic record or teaching skills. He seemed to care more about his religion and the fact that he'd traveled to the Far East. The closer he got to the campus, the more he grew concerned that he'd been had.

"I was assured a new college was being created in California," he said years later. "The only problem was, I couldn't find Long Beach State College." He and his wife stayed in a hotel on the first night. When he finally came to campus, he noticed a "library" consisting of small buildings the size of three offices. "I thought, 'My God, what have I gotten into? There are no books.'"

There were no books to speak of for at least a couple of months. Classes started on September 28, 1949, in a converted apartment in what is now the tony neighborhood of Park Estates. It was far from tony then. The area was

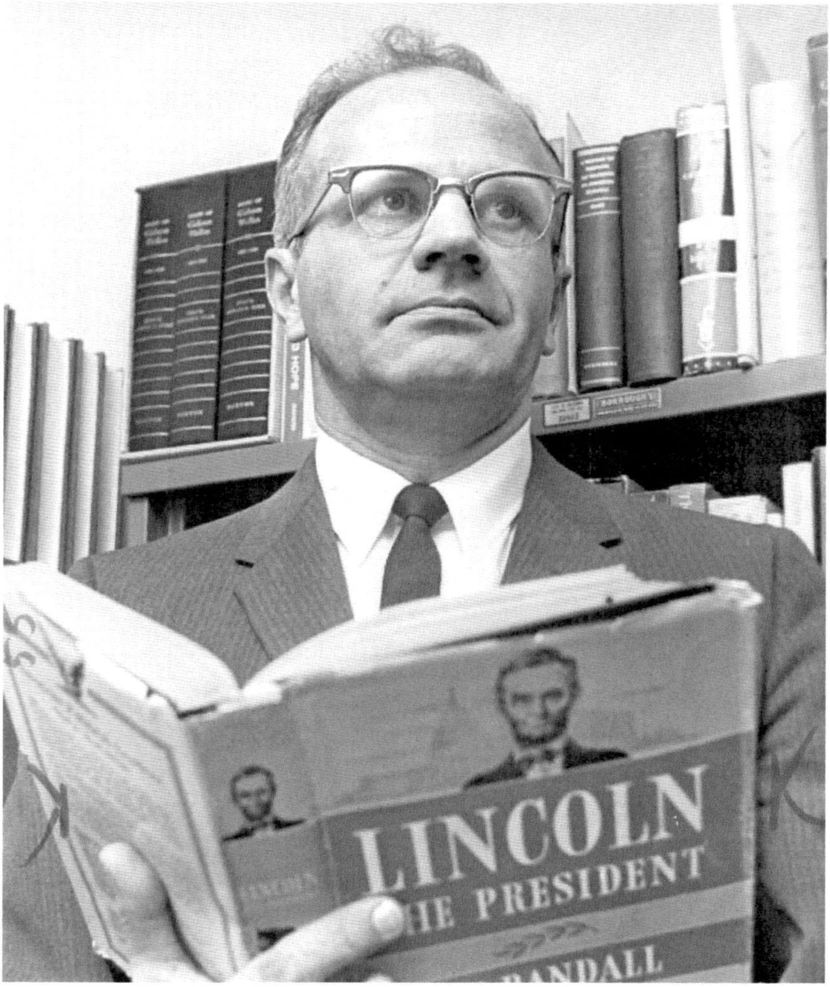

Professor Irving Ahlquist, pictured here in 1962, was a popular history professor who had his doubts when he arrived in September 1949. *Courtesy of the* Long Beach Press-Telegram.

so new that, on some days, construction workers outnumbered the students. But 169 students did register for classes that fall, and administrators were thrilled to get that many.

One of them was Isabel Patterson, who would go on to a career in real estate and philanthropy. The Texas native, who worked in the navy during World War II and later moved to the Long Beach area, read about the new college in the newspaper. A little ashamed she never got her degree at Texas Tech, she went to apply. She was told to go to a fruit stand on Pacific Coast

Highway at Anaheim Street, and someone there directed her to the sixteen-unit apartment building.

The biggest classes were held in living rooms, middle-sized classes were in the dining rooms and the smallest classes were in the kitchen. Music education students stored their music and instruments in the bathroom. Patterson remembers seeing construction workers everywhere, while students moved through "classrooms" to get to the bathroom.

A makeshift canteen fashioned from a converted washroom served mostly "Miller sandwiches," which the many World War II veterans on hand remembered as two dry pieces of bread and a thin slice of ham or some other meat wrapped in paper and sold for fifteen cents. The canteen also sold doughnuts, soda and coffee. It was primitive—a far different student experience than that of the storied institutions to the north—the University of Southern California (USC) and the University of California, Los Angeles (UCLA). Before Long Beach State opened in 1949 and Los Angeles State College in 1947, students in Southern California had limited choices for affordable higher education.

But after World War II, millions of veterans converged on college campuses, thanks to the GI Bill. And the end of amped-up wartime production meant a newly unleashed workforce ready, in large measure, to get a college education.

For one local family, college wasn't even on the radar. Beverly Lewis's family never discussed it, and her father urged her to learn typing instead. USC and UCLA were out of the question. Lewis, later to become Beverly O'Neill, would go on to become a popular three-term mayor of Long

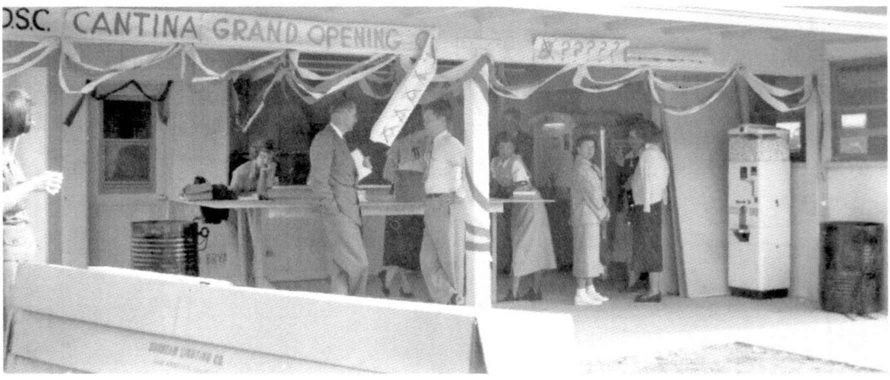

The first canteen eatery—coffee, doughnuts and Miller sandwiches were served out of a converted washroom. *Courtesy of the University Archives.*

Beach. She started out at Long Beach City College before transferring to Long Beach State.

"Long Beach City College and Long Beach State was an answer I had at the time—and the only one—because there just wasn't funding to go someplace where it was going to be costly," O'Neill said.

Long Beach State's September 28 opening was postponed by numerous construction delays. "Gestalt theory was filtered through the sounds of jackhammers and Skilsaws," according to a *Long Beach Press-Telegram* account published in the first yearbook. Professors and students stepped over lumber, paint buckets and tarpaulins on their way to registration and class.

A chronic shortage of typewriters and office equipment at the new school meant delays in ordering important items such as books. Even the book budget was "lost in the bureaucratic mill in Sacramento" until November, when the first book purchase was approved, according to an unpublished history of the college by Kaye Briegel and David Bernstein.

The temporary library was completed by November 10, but the first book did not come in until December 6, which was, the college history noted dryly, "a red-letter day for the library."

The librarian, Charles Boorkman, stored what books he could get his hands on in his own apartment. Book donations from the community were kept in garbage can lockers.

When the library moved into temporary buildings on the new campus, shelves quickly filled with new and secondhand books. Books and magazines liberated from "dead storage" were piled in a large heap on the floor. It looked, according to a college history published in 1959, "more like the unveiling of King Tut's tomb than a contemporary library."

Books weren't the only things that were scarce. Physical education students, lacking equipment and facilities, played "Ring Around the Rosie" for exercise. The *Forty-Niner* student newspaper started publishing on November 11 as a mimeographed sheet produced in a toolshed with a leaky roof.

Students, toughened by war and the rationing of meat, metal and gasoline that went with it, took these new privations in stride.

"You felt you were a pioneer," said Patterson.

Boorkman said later that it was "difficult—if not impossible—to re-create the excitement and verve of which all concerned with the establishment of the college carried out their tasks." It was like erecting a circus tent, he said, with the same organized confusion.

And there were benefits to being "stuck in this one little area" of dust, makeshift buildings and construction debris, said O'Neill, who graduated

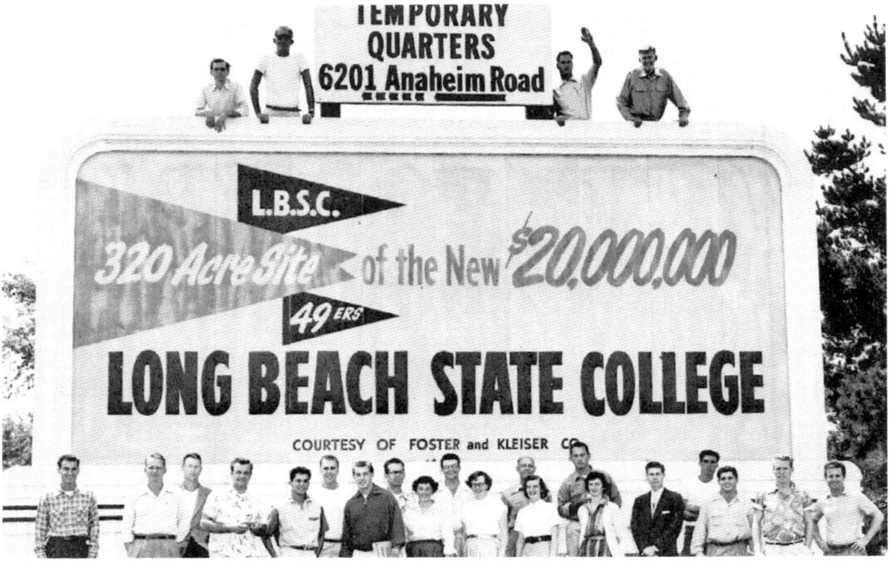

Students in the early 1950s show their enthusiasm for the new college going up on the outskirts of town. *Courtesy of CSULB.*

in 1952. Professors and students saw each other every morning in the canteen. They ate lunch together. The students and faculty enjoyed a sense of camaraderie that was never recaptured after the campus population exploded in the 1950s, '60s and '70s.

"I can't tell you how much I enjoyed going out there," Patterson would say later, "because classes were small; professors, we all knew them…It was such a friendly, close school."

O'Neill said when she and her husband—Bill O'Neill, who was in the first graduating class—got married, her professors came to the wedding. "I felt like we were building something," she said. "It was exciting; we were in on the beginning of something that was going to grow."

That the new college was able to open its doors at all was a small miracle that took hard work, luck and some last-minute help from an eager and enterprising local developer.

2

The Story of Long Beach State

"I Can Tear Out Partitions as Easily as I Can Put Them In"

In early 1949, two memorable events affecting Long Beach happened in quick succession. On January 28, snow fell—a "mantel of white" falling on several parts of the city—during a rare month of bitterly cold southland weather. The next day, the California legislature, citing an "urgent need," called for the establishment of a state college to serve southeastern Los Angeles and Orange Counties at the "earliest possible moment."

With the passage of the bill, signed into law by Governor Earl Warren, things started moving quickly. The words "urgency" or "urgent" were mentioned seven times in the two-page Assembly Bill No. 8. It's not hard to see why. UCLA and USC were filled to capacity with newly liberated servicemen and women, GI Bill benefits in hand. Bean fields, orange fields and vacant lots were quickly being plowed under to make way for the endless grid of tract homes now so familiar to Southern Californians.

Bill No. 8, however, provided no land and no money. Not yet. P. Victor Peterson, who had gotten Los Angeles State College going in 1947, had been recruited to be the president of the college, which was to be located someplace in southeastern Los Angeles or in Orange County.

Peterson was asked to do the same for the new institution. He was part of a site team made up of state and local officials who drove from the Palos Verdes Peninsula to Santa Ana and viewed fifteen sites. They looked at Lakewood, Downey, Santa Ana and Norwalk. The Irvine Company offered 160 acres for a college as long as it wasn't on the coast.

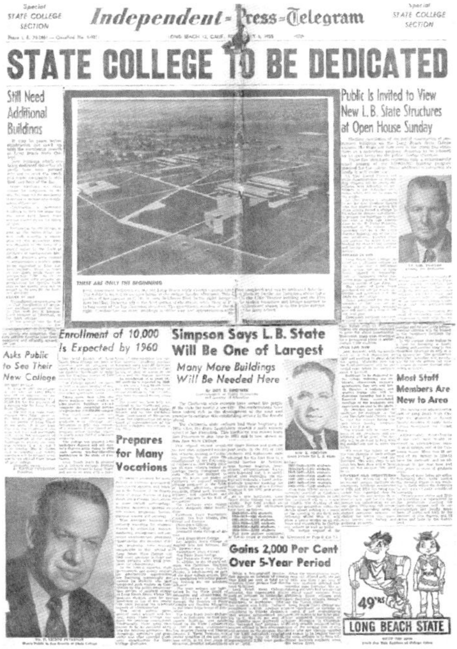

Special STATE COLLEGE SECTION

Independent-Press-Telegram

STATE COLLEGE TO BE DEDICATED

Still Need Additional Buildings

Public Is Invited to View New L.B. State Structures at Open House Sunday

Enrollment of 10,000 Is Expected by 1960

Simpson Says L.B. State Will Be One of Largest

Many More Buildings Will Be Needed Here

Asks Public to See Their New College

Most Staff Members Are New to Area

Prepares for Many Vocations

Gains 2,000 Per Cent Over 5-Year Period

LONG BEACH STATE

The *Long Beach Independent Press-Telegram* rolled out a Long Beach State special section in 1955. *Courtesy of the Historical Society of Long Beach.*

The selection committee members independently ranked their choices from one to fifteen and put them in a hat. To everyone's astonishment, all agreed on their first choice: a gently sloping, 322-acre site on the outskirts of Long Beach, next to the Long Beach Naval Hospital.

But there was one problem. The parcel's owner, Fred Bixby, had no interest in a deal. He already had plans to subdivide the property. But Assemblyman William Grant, who was keen to have a college built in his district, spoke to Bixby. The two men, who were friends, finally came to an agreement, and Bixby held off developing the land until state and local officials could work some magic.

Peterson and Aubrey Douglass, the state associate superintendent for public instruction, met with state and local officials, including the head of the Long Beach Chamber of Commerce, and local developer Lloyd Whaley. An ambitious, energetic and shrewd businessman, Whaley was in the process of converting vast swaths of eastern Long Beach into one- and two-bedroom starter homes.

State officials were having a difficult time finding a temporary site to get a skeleton institution going. Douglass wanted to find an existing structure suitable for a starter site. The men drove all over the two-lane roads through land being cleared for new houses, trying to find something suitable. They stopped to cool their heels in Whaley's construction office on Anaheim Road in Park Estates, which was still filled with trees and scrub but had begun to sprout some half-finished apartment buildings. Whaley remarked that he had several apartments under construction, and he'd be "tickled to death to turn them over." When Douglass asked Whaley how much he'd charge, Whaley told him whatever price he set would be just fine with him. Peterson later recalled in an oral interview that "Douglass looked at him so funny and said, 'Nobody ever talked to a state man like that before. They always want to gouge the state.'"

Then, Orange County officials launched a furious last-minute push for the college. Orange County legislators managed to get the state attorney general to rule that the $125,000 in seed money—legislators had earlier killed a bill for a more reasonable $800,000—could not be doled out without his approval.

As it happened, the attorney general was in Mexico on vacation until August 25, 1949. That didn't leave much time for the approval and construction of a college for the fall semester—even a temporary one.

But on August 25, Peterson got the call. The deal was on, and he would get the seed money for the temporary college. Peterson then called Whaley, who, thinking the plan was off, had proceeded to construct his Park Estates apartment houses. When Peterson asked if it was too late, Whaley replied, "I can tear out partitions as easily as I can put them in."

For the next month, Whaley steered carpenters, painters, plumbers and electricians to eight two-bedroom apartments, aiming to transform them into classrooms and offices. Garages became science and art labs, and the laundry became the college canteen. Months later, Whaley would be offering professors discounts to move into his new Park Estates neighborhood.

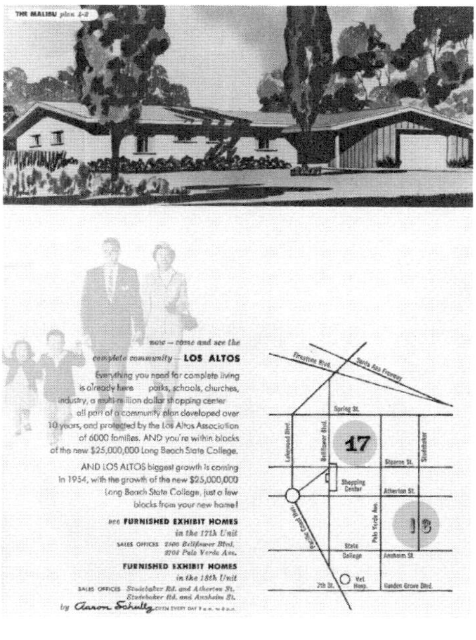

Lloyd Whaley, who practically gave the college its first temporary quarters, also promoted the new college as a centerpiece in his booming eastside developments. *Courtesy of the Historical Society of Long Beach.*

At 7:00 a.m. on September 27, Whaley joined state and local officials and a dozen faculty members at the new college. The faculty members held their first meeting under a pepper tree. Professors helped out, using picks and shovels to clear away enough construction debris to permit the first group of 169 students to register for classes.

The new college would initially admit only upper division students. Since no one knew for sure where

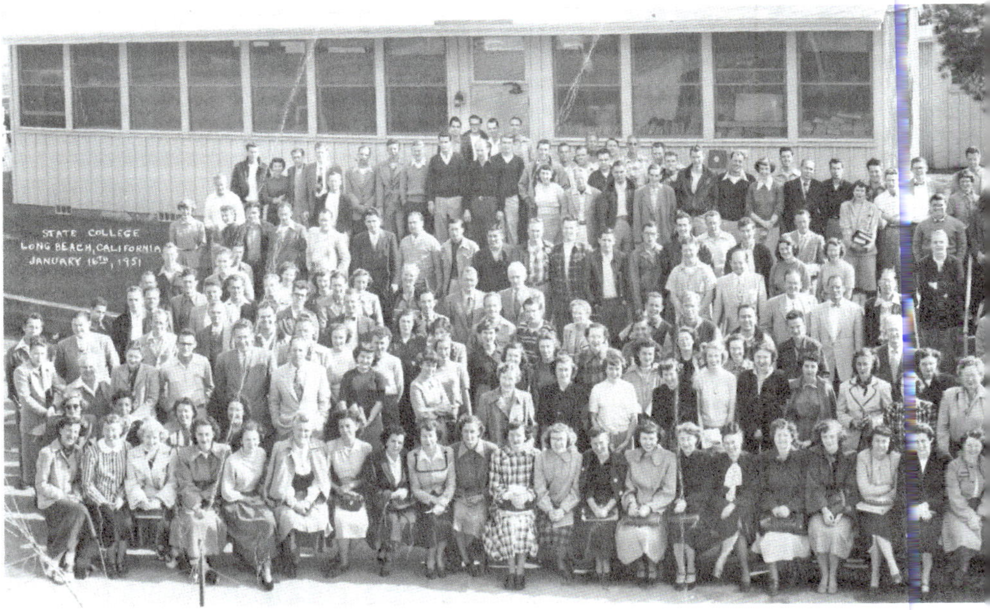
STATE COLLEGE
LONG BEACH, CALIFORNIA
JANUARY 16TH, 1951

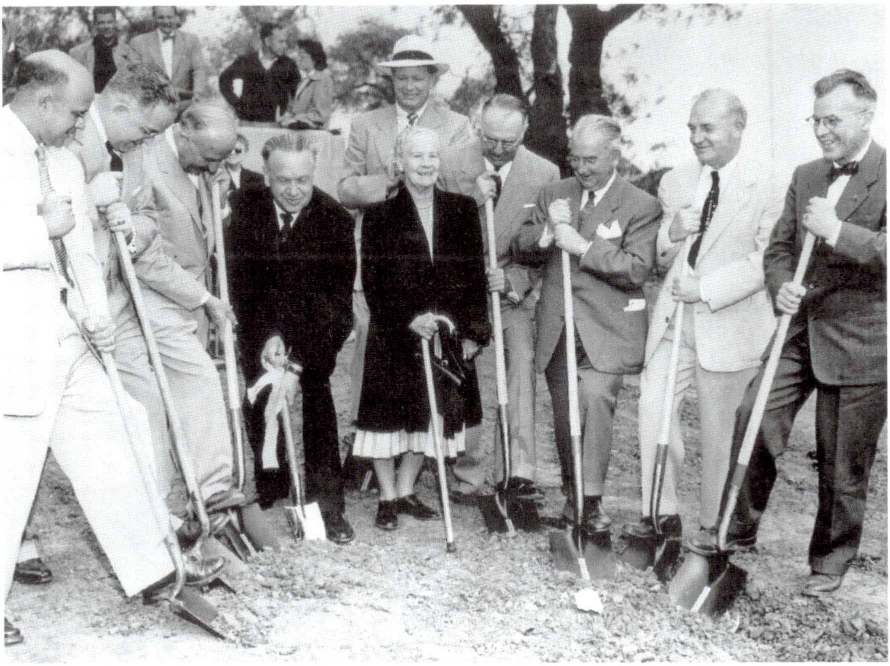

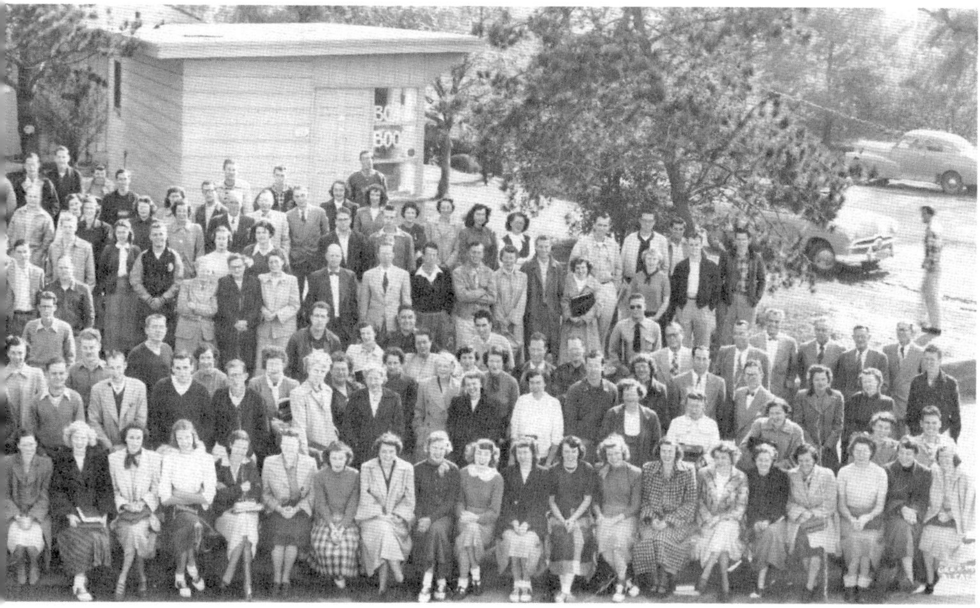

Above: One of the first class photos, taken in 1951, next to the converted Park Estates apartments. *Courtesy of Beverly O'Neill.*

Opposite, bottom: Groundbreaking for permanent buildings in May 1953. The college's first president, P. Victor Peterson, is fourth from left, and Florence Green Bixby, the wife of original landowner Fred Bixby, is on Peterson's left. *Courtesy of the University Archives.*

the new school would ultimately end up, it was given the placeholder name of Los Angeles–Orange County State College. Instruction centered on teacher training, partly because public schools were springing up all over the area and partly because such training didn't demand many resources that the fledgling institution just couldn't provide.

It was a big victory but a temporary one. The real celebration came in June 1950, when Long Beach voters, by a 10–1 margin, approved a plan to use $1 million in oil money to purchase the 320-acre site just east of the first temporary apartment site. In the meantime, Orange County voters rejected a similar measure to finance a state college. Orange County had to wait until 1957 to get its state school in Fullerton.

The temporary college in Park Estates was immediately renamed Long Beach State College, and plans were put in place to build temporary and then permanent structures on "Fred Bixby's bean fields." Peterson's daughter, Ellie Johnson, remembers riding in a car with Peterson and two of the new college deans and listening to them sing happy songs on the drive.

Lloyd Whaley was happy, too—about the impact the new college would have on his booming developments. Three years later, he would write in the *Long Beach Press-Telegram*, "With the advent of Long Beach State College into the Los Altos Village community, the future of this area was assured [*sic*]." He added that the college would boost home values and add so much "cultural charm and prestige" that people would eventually "compare it with Westwood Village and nearby UCLA."

The new school needed faculty, lots of faculty. Peterson had brought ten faculty members from Los Angeles State College with him and hired two others. Soon he would be flying to Iowa, Missouri, Harvard and Columbia to find newly minted professors willing to take a chance at a new institution in a booming region with predictably perfect weather.

College officials were elated, and the students were excited. The first decade was a time of opportunity and exponential growth and, with it, came growing pains and strife.

3

P. Victor Peterson

"He Was a Builder"

P. Victor Peterson favored double-breasted suits and hated to have his picture taken. He also wasn't much of a public speaker. A hardworking Iowa native with a serious mien, he did not seem like the man to launch the seat-of-the-pants enterprise that was Long Beach State.

But he did. The former chemistry professor, who would go on to write books on California trees, became best known for making sure piles of dead ones would quickly grow into a temporary, then a permanent, college in Long Beach.

"If there was one guy you could imagine not being an effective fundraiser, it was Peterson," said Lee Brown, a journalism professor who was the *Forty-Niner* editor in the late '50s and later worked for the university. "He seemed more at home in a lab. But he was a builder."

When Peterson started as president in 1949, 169 students were crammed into a converted apartment building. When he retired in 1959, close to 10,000 attend classes on a sprawling Long Beach State College campus in a city that was growing like wildfire.

A big man at five feet, eleven inches with large features and an aversion to getting his photo taken—librarians at the university archives are hard-put to find a portrait of him—he was also a strong family man and a good listener, said his daughter, Ellie Johnson. "He was very interested in what people had to say. He was perceptive about people's character and quite kind."

"President Pete" was well known to students, especially in the early days when faculty, administrators and students shared meals and generally

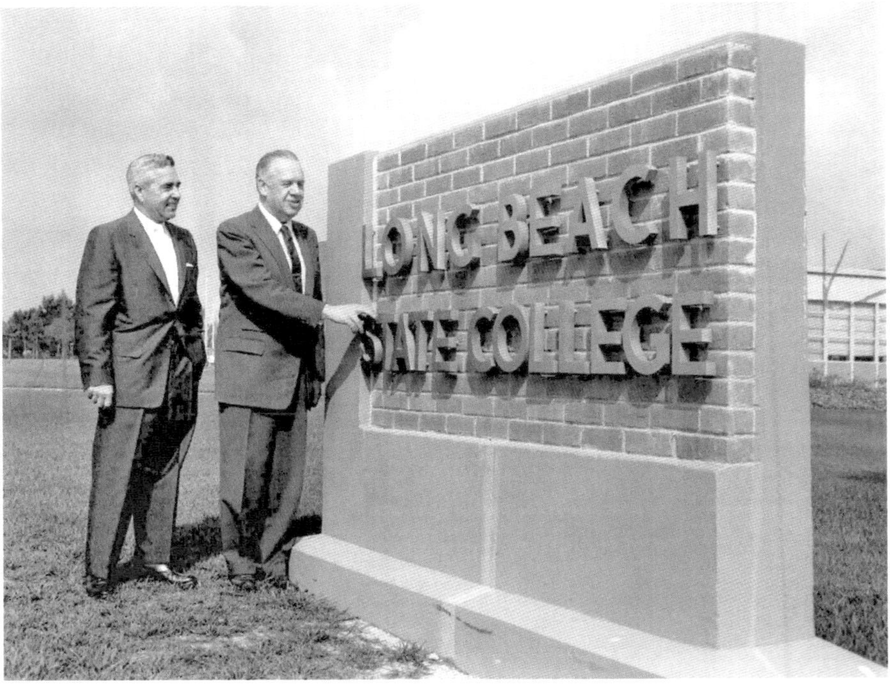

Lloyd Whaley presents President P. Victor Peterson with a $1,000 stone marker for the college entrance in 1958. Peterson started the seed work in engaging the community in the new college. *Courtesy of the* Long Beach Press-Telegram.

close quarters in two temporary apartments. They named the 49er mascot "Prospector Pete" after him.

Peterson also worked Sacramento officials to get more state attention and resources. When they questioned his budget requests, Peterson reminded them that there were as many people living within a twenty-mile radius of campus as were to be found in Washington, Oregon and Utah combined. Then, he'd ask how many colleges could be found in those states. Several. He generally got more money after that.

Peterson taught chemistry and agriculture in his native Iowa before moving to San Jose State in 1922. He became dean of the college there and founded the West Coast Nature School, leading excursions to study birds, trees and geology. Johnson said Peterson, as dean, insisted on teaching the freshman-level chemistry class himself because he was concerned it was becoming a "flunk out" class.

Peterson also chaired the San Jose city planning commission from 1939 to 1947, and his daughter believes his planning experience factored into the selection of the Long Beach State college site—including the fact that it was set on a hill on the outskirts of town.

State officials, reacting to anticipated postwar growth in California, tapped Peterson to launch Los Angeles State College in 1947.

Peterson said later in an oral history that he was sitting in the science office at San Jose in the spring of 1947 when he got a call from the associate superintendent of public instruction saying that he was going to pick Peterson up and the two would drive to Los Angeles. Peterson balked at first but later said that state officials knew "I had been at San Jose for twenty-five years and so I was pretty thoroughly familiar with that, pretty familiar with the boys in Sacramento, as well as the state department of education."

Peterson said he could have stayed in Los Angeles but didn't like the way city officials sought to control the college there. So when he was asked to

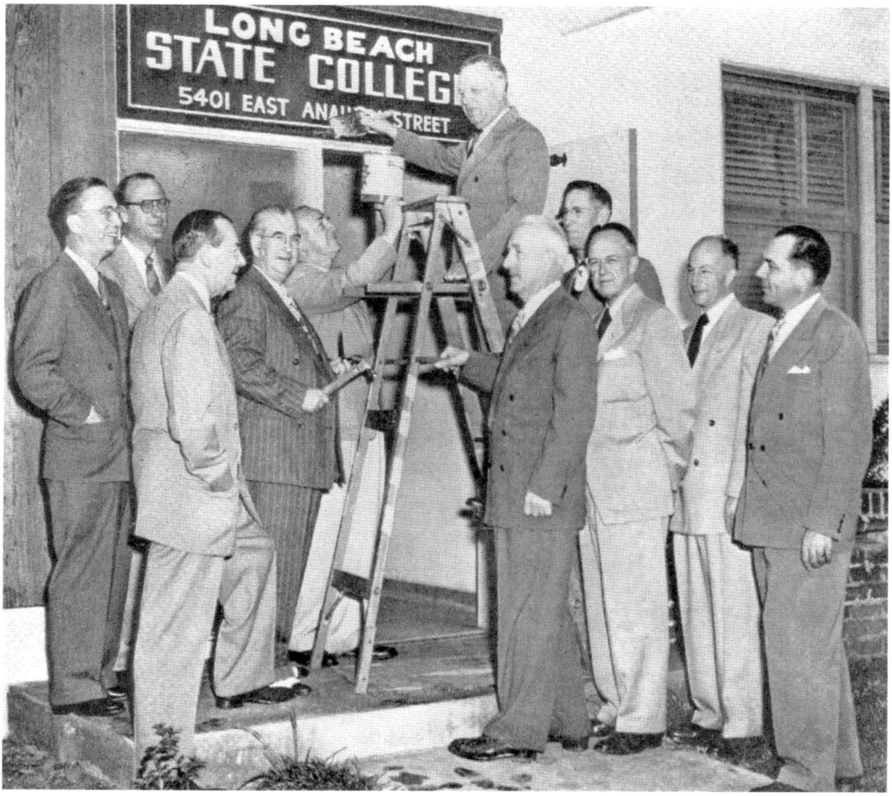

Peterson and fellow administrators pose by the new college sign shortly after voters in June 1950 approve a referendum to use oil money to buy the land for the college. *Courtesy of the University Archives.*

help launch Long Beach State, he said he found the city's hands-off support more to his liking. Johnson said that a San Jose State administrator once told her that her dad "could run General Motors."

Indeed, Peterson, who was fifty-seven when he took over in Long Beach, ruled the campus with a strong hand. He personally hired faculty, and all decisions went through his office. For a time, administrators even approved articles that went in the *Forty-Niner* student newspaper.

Students recall a president who cared deeply about the college and its students but who also remained rather formal. C.J. Klug, who graduated with his bachelor's in 1954 in business administration, said, "When he came by, you hid. He wasn't a bad person, [but] you felt like you might get in trouble if you did something wrong."

Peterson told incoming faculty straight up that Long Beach State was not a research institution and that those who believed otherwise should teach elsewhere, according to a letter that history professor Richard Wilde wrote to a friend in September 1951. Peterson felt professors should focus all their time on the classroom and students. Francis "Frenchy" Flynn, a longtime dean at the college in the 1950s and '60s, said later that Peterson and most administrators at the time believed the state colleges should be "basically geared to the vocational and the occupational" and that

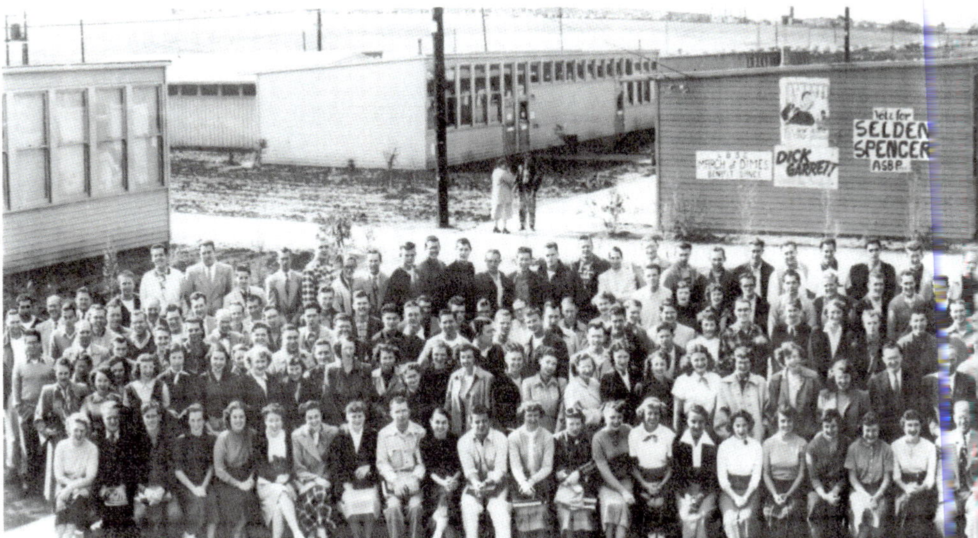

The Long Beach State student body in 1952 in front of the temporary buildings on the new campus. *Courtesy of Beverly O'Neill.*

research and advanced degrees should largely be left to the University of California schools such as those in Berkeley and Los Angeles.

History professor Irving Ahlquist said that Peterson favored general education and told him that he'd "like to have someone who perhaps would pump my gas for me and tell me a little about India and a little about China."

It was a vision that jibed with a strong faction of the politically powerful state board of education, which regulated and approved budgets for colleges and public schools. The new college system was a top-down operation in those days—and Sacramento was at the very top. All requests went through the imperious Department of Finance, which had veto power over expenses at the new, growing state schools.

Long Beach State would later embrace shared governance, placing the school's faculty in the first few rows of campus hiring and decision-making. But that was not how the school worked in the 1950s. Peterson's top-down structure might have made sense in the days when the front office was small, support staff was almost nonexistent and hiring was conducted at a breathless pace. There was also the fact that the entire college had to be planned and constructed.

But professors, recruited from all over the country and raised on the "publish or perish" ethos, chafed at Peterson's view of higher education.

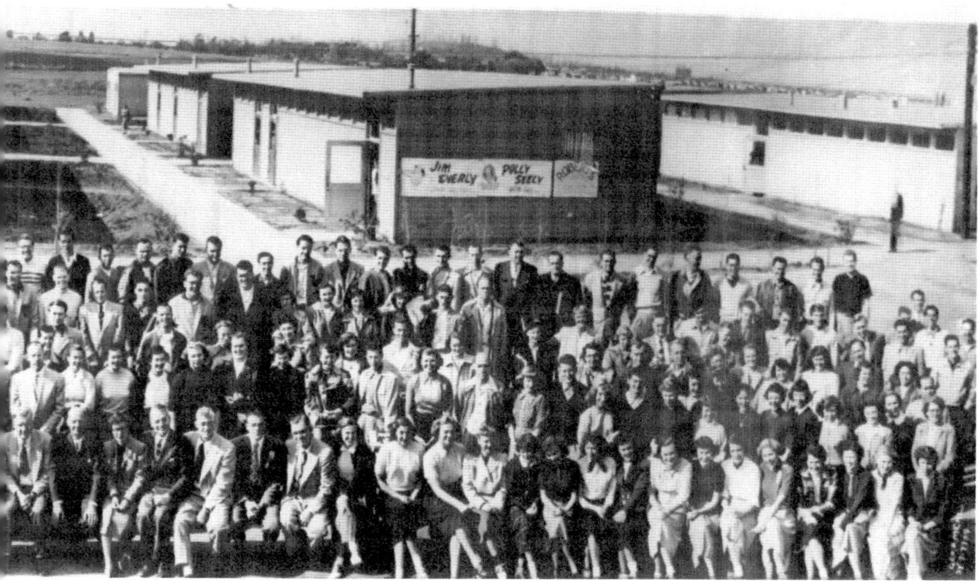

The young faculty believed that research made teaching more relevant and current. As the 1950s rolled on, they were becoming increasingly restive. Many sought a more ambitious curriculum beyond that of broad survey courses and vocational pursuits. They were World War II veterans who had seen plenty during their time abroad and were in no mood to be given marching orders from what they viewed as an autocratic administration. That administration, under the gun to build a campus, was increasingly butting heads with a faculty made up of some of the brightest and most adventurous—willing to cross the country to join a college no one had heard of. It was a perfect storm for acrimony.

Then things got ugly.

By 1959, almost 60 percent of faculty members, whom Peterson mostly hired himself, decided they wanted him to resign. Peterson charged that a "left-wing element" had infiltrated faculty, while the faculty said people were being dismissed on trumped-up charges for the crime of daring to challenge the administration.

Bill O'Neill, a student in the college's first class who returned to teach in the late 1950s, later described an atmosphere of professors "locked in offices, drinking coffee and smoking and plotting against the administration." By then, the fight was drawing the notice of the *Los Angeles Times*, twenty-five miles away. One headline read, "LBSC Prexy Under Fire, Won't Quit." More importantly, the campus brouhaha was getting attention from Sacramento as professors went north to complain about Peterson in person.

Peterson eventually retired on June 30, 1959, at age sixty-seven. Flynn, the former dean, said later that, though he supported Peterson's decisions, administrators at the college in the 1950s "were probably not bringing faculty into the decision-making as well as we should have, I'm sure of that."

Acrimony cooled in the early '60s under the presidency of Carl McIntosh, a gifted speaker—though certain faculty members counted comma splices in McIntosh's convocation speech. Rancor cooled as the campus matured and adopted a faculty council and academic senate; "shared governance" took hold in the 1960s. But the campus battles would continue under future presidents, including Stephen Horn, in the '60s, '70s and '80s. And the teaching-versus-research tension at the university, as well as at other California state colleges, continues to this day as professors struggle to complete research under steep teaching loads. Richard Wilde, one of the professors most staunchly opposed to Peterson's policies, wrote that, while he gave Peterson credit for using his knowledge of a complex state system to "build a California state college out of nothing...He was definitely right in insisting that faculty give first priority to teaching, though wrong in denigrating scholarship and research." Wilde added that Peterson "rightly aimed to avoid an undergraduate education evident at major universities where faculty, focused on research, had little direct contact with undergraduates."

Peterson lived another twenty years and remained active in college and city affairs. He died in 1979, at age eighty-seven. Then-president Stephen Horn commented that Peterson "had the dedication and energy to begin soundly a great university and to live to see it well under way in meeting the needs of a diverse regional, national and international population. We will sorely miss his care and involvement."

4

Parking

"Spanish Broom and Mustard Grass and Ford Falcons"

Students born a couple of generations after the founding of Long Beach State are used to roaring through four-level parking structures. Or they might idle behind a pedestrian walking through a full lot, hoping the stranger will take off and vacate a space.

It's a simple formula of too many students and not quite enough parking spots. Another factor, as the real estate agents might say, is location. The parking lots and garages are on the northerly lower campus, and most classes are on upper campus, where parking slots are even scarcer.

Parking was free or nearly free on the Long Beach State campus of yore. Land was plentiful; about 20 of the 320 acres were occupied by barracks-like temporary buildings and a few under-construction permanent ones. The rest was open scrub and old farm fields. Sheep grazed where the Pyramid is now. With the prairie-like setting, one might think parking would have been the least of these education pioneers' concerns. But no.

In the days before the 405 Freeway blasted through the east side of Long Beach, students drove to school along Seventh Street and Pacific Coast Highway. DeSotos, Edsels and Buick Roadmasters were parked along Seventh Street and, later, on dirt lots on the side of a hill near where the Student Union is now. No big deal. Cars and dirt were a frequent pairing in those days; Palo Verde Avenue was a dirt road until the 1960s. This situation was fine on most sunny California days. But when it rained, those DeSotos, Edsels and Roadmasters got stuck.

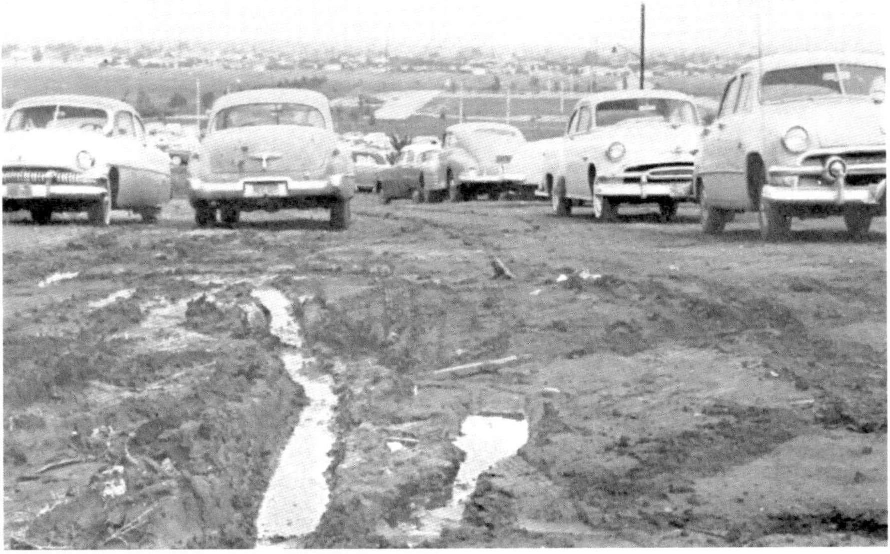

When the rains came, mud flowed and cars would bump and slide into one another. Here is a view of the cars looking down toward lower campus. *Courtesy of CSULB.*

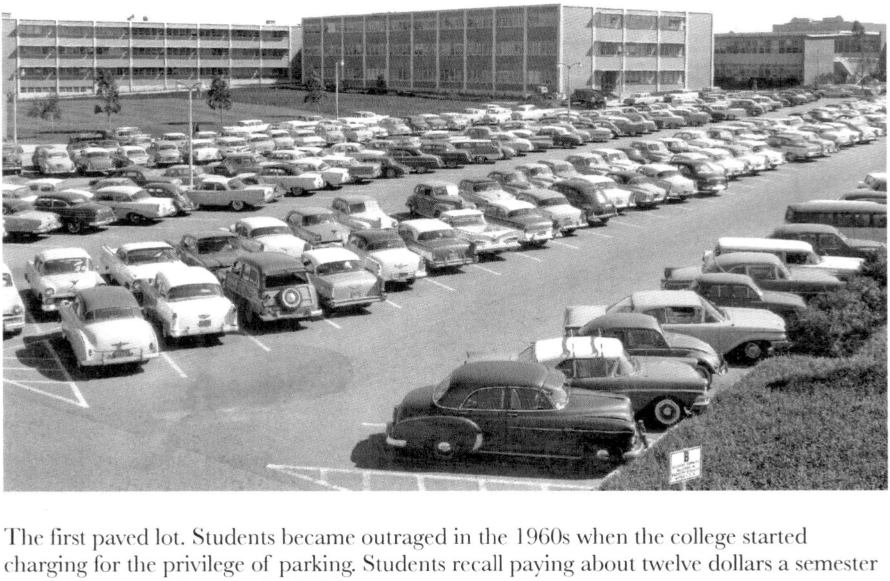

The first paved lot. Students became outraged in the 1960s when the college started charging for the privilege of parking. Students recall paying about twelve dollars a semester in the late 1960s. *Courtesy of CSULB.*

The *Forty-Niner* newspaper reported in November 1951 that President P. Victor Peterson helped students whose cars had gotten mired along Anaheim Street. "Dr. Peterson, in a business suit that was neat and pressed at the start of the evening, pitched in with Lloyd McClung, head janitor, and using a pickup truck, the two pushed and pulled the bogged-down autos free of the mud."

And when the rain turned into torrents, the mud and water rose, and cars bumped and crashed into each other like a slow-moving demolition derby, sliding down the hill toward the area that is now Brotman Hall.

Beverly O'Neill, later Long Beach mayor, remembers dashing out of class to save her friend's car. "One car would come down, and there would be this maze of cars sliding down," she said. "One would slide and then the other one would slide." It was a messy affair and students complained lustily about it to professors and one another.

Long Beach State was no different from colleges across the country that tried to corral the parking on a booming campus. The school grew from just under ten thousand students in 1960 to twenty-one thousand by 1968. Campus master plans and enrollment projections were created and then pushed aside as inadequate. Parking was the same way—administrators couldn't build lots, or find space for them, fast enough.

The college even turned to the military, tapping a retired World War II brigadier general, Francis Day, to wage war on the campus parking problem. On his first day of work, the general wanted to get a look at the campus. He phoned transportation and said, "This is Brigadier General Day. Send me my car!" There was a flurry of activity as the folks in transportation tried to figure out how to break it to the general that this wasn't the military, and there would be no car or driver available to be brought 'round.

Finally, President Carl McIntosh walked down the hall and explained the situation—if the general wanted to drive around campus, he'd have to use his own car. Day actually turned out to be a genial fellow and drew plans for gravel and paved lots to ease the problem. Few of them came to fruition.

Students found their own solutions. They avoided the fees and hassle by leaving their cars on weedy dirt lots south of campus by Seventh Street near Bellflower Boulevard—lots occupied by drugstores, restaurants and car washes today. The college was charging for parking by the 1960s. The twelve-dollar-per-semester fee put a big pothole in the budget of a student paying sixty dollars per month for rent, said 1968 grad John Stacy. The parking situation involved "lots of Spanish broom and mustard grass and Ford Falcons," he recalled.

Planners talked of building a parking garage on Seventh Street by upper campus, where spots are still hard to come by. But that plan was scrapped for fear of angering neighbors living near the college's southern border. Eventually, four garages went up on lower campus near the Pyramid and Palo Verde Avenue.

No dirt lots ring the campus anymore. Students park in the nearby neighborhoods and walk or skateboard to class. Neighbors impose parking restrictions, and students just start parking a few blocks away. It's a classic problem of a college spilling over its borders and onto streets filled with mid-century homes with one-car garages, narrow driveways and fed-up neighbors wanting the extra curb space for their own surplus cars.

The university has tried to coax students from their cars by contracting with Long Beach Transit so that students can ride the city bus to school for free. There are more bike lanes on and around campus. Shuttles roam the campus to bring students from their cars to their classes, but using them takes time and planning, which can be in short supply for twenty-something students. They still complain indignantly to one another on social media and in the school newspaper. The campus has changed, but in many ways, parking hasn't.

"We had almost no parking," recalled Dana Rohrabacher, a history major who graduated in 1969. "I ended up with a four-year degree, and I tell people it was really a five-year degree because I spent a year looking for a parking place."

5

The Campus

Join the Peach Corps and Other Missions

When Carl McIntosh, the college's second president, first laid eyes on ten-year-old Long Beach State in 1959, he was mostly underwhelmed. He said in an unpublished campus history that his "first impression of the campus was that there had been a lot of money spent to create a deliberate impression of economy without the reality of it. There were some buildings here, which were almost deliberately made to look ugly, so they would look cheap."

Despite these shortcomings, McIntosh said, he thought Long Beach State had the potential to become a beautiful campus. But it was hard to see beauty in 1950s and '60s Long Beach State. There were temporary classrooms that looked like military barracks. Students caught whiffs of sewer smells as they slogged through muddy parking in the marshy, treeless lower campus and strolled across makeshift wooden bridges. The upper campus was similarly stark, dotted with drab mid-century concrete buildings.

Students and professors cheered when the first permanent buildings went up in the mid-1950s. The early structures—the science buildings that became the Peterson buildings, the fine arts building and the liberal arts buildings—were part of a campus plan drawn up by state-funded, often politically connected architects. Former facilities head Scott Charmack described it as a McDonald's-like approach to architecture: "They took a crummy design and did it everywhere."

Stephen Horn, who became president in 1970, later called the Peterson science buildings "a mess of cement." The structure "contained so much

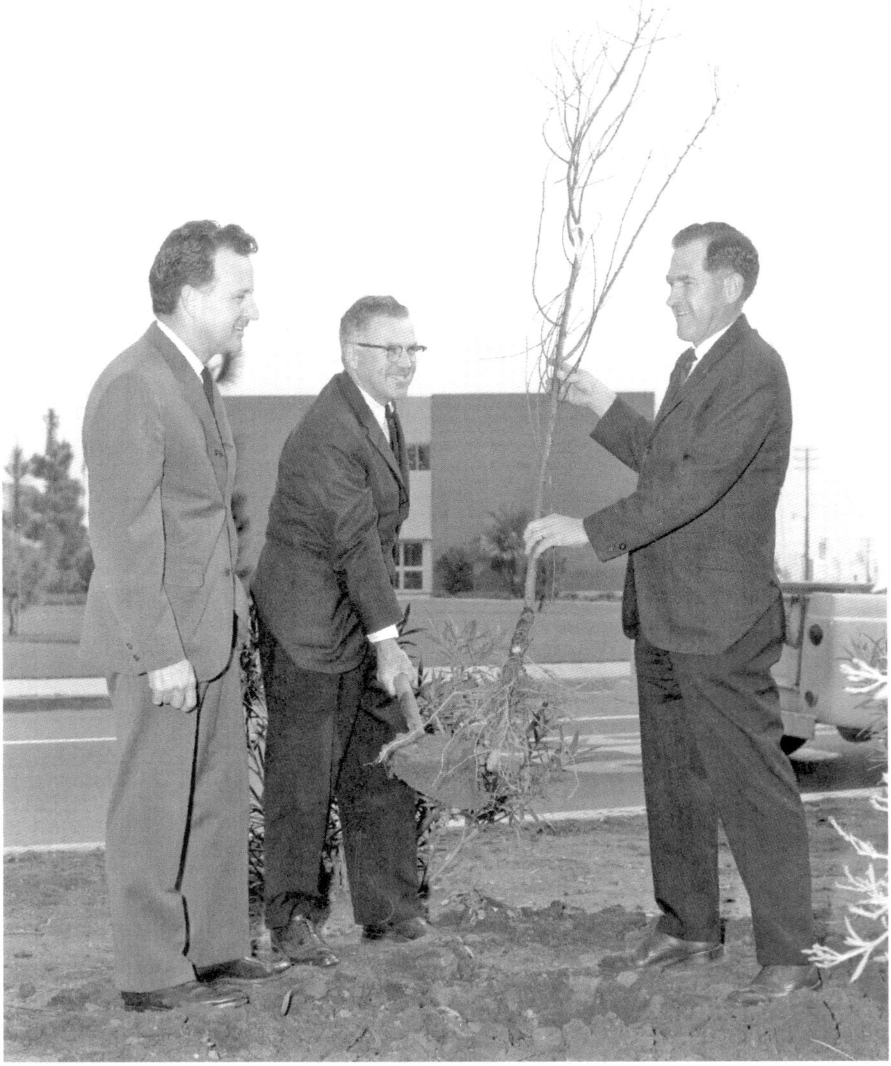

Architect Ed Killingsworth, dean of students Francis "Frenchy" Flynn and landscape architect Ed Lovell (right) launch the peach tree campaign in 1965. *Courtesy of the University Archives.*

cement that we concluded the damn thing would be around a hundred years from now…A horrible mess."

But the campus aesthetics could have been a lot worse. Today, there are trees, lush grass and new lawns of drought-tolerant vegetation. There is still plenty of concrete, but now there are also dappled-light walkways with views from the top of the once-barren hill.

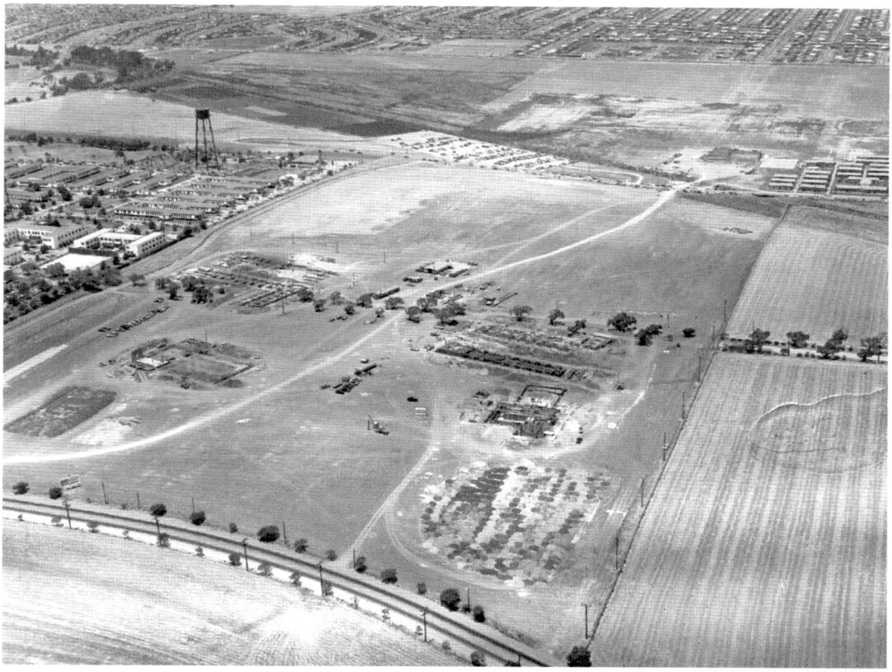

The college's upper campus, circa 1952. In the left-hand corner are the very beginnings of the one-story administration building, which would later become an education building; (clockwise from left) the library; Liberal Arts 2 and 3; Fine Arts 1 and 2; and the music building. Anaheim Road still cuts through the center of campus. The temporary buildings are in the far right corner. *Courtesy of the University Archives.*

Long Beach State might never enjoy USC's ivy-covered structures financed by old-money benefactors, but it developed a look of its own. For that, campus denizens must give credit to a few key factors. The longtime dean of development, Francis "Frenchy" Flynn, was an architect trained at USC, and he loved red brick. In the mid-1950s, the state—the Department of Finance controlled all state college construction in those days—insisted on using cost-saving cement. Flynn lobbied Sacramento officials so hard that they finally agreed to his requests, mostly to get him off the phone. Flynn said in an oral history that they weren't going for ivy, exactly, but just a little red brick to soften the penitentiary look.

So they put a bit of brick on the sides of the Peterson and the liberal arts buildings. It wasn't much, and the buildings were still drab, but it started a standard that the campus architects followed. The state, in the early days, went grudgingly along, as Flynn remembered in an interview with former president Stephen Horn:

We were the envy of others at that time. My colleagues were all asking "How did you get it?" San Jose was getting monolithic buildings…"How do you get brick. Finance won't listen to us," they asked. Of course, once we got it, it established what we call a building materials palette, and we stayed with it.

THE SIGNAL HILL OIL BOOM

In June 1921, Los Alamitos Well No. 1 let loose with a one-hundred-foot gusher of oil, marking an era that would draw thousands of workers to Long Beach, including the oilman father of Ed Killingsworth.

Young Killingsworth had an early interest in painting but turned to architecture and studied at USC. He quickly made a name for himself when he helped design some of the Case Study homes—simple, economical and well-designed California homes created during a campaign launched by the editor of *Art & Architecture* magazine. At the same time, the state was pivoting away from top-down control of college campus aesthetics.

In 1961, a board of trustees took control of California state colleges, including Long Beach State. No longer would the college be required to use the state's in-house architects. The colleges would be permitted to find their own promising professionals, preferably with a connection to the college's home city. In 1961, the trustees turned to Killingsworth.

The forty-five-year-old and his firm—Killingsworth, Brady, Smith and Associates—drew up a 1963 master plan for Long Beach State that called for a unified look to make the campus more friendly for pedestrians. Some suggestions came to pass—city officials agreed to condemn old Anaheim Street, which bisected the campus. The architects also suggested that instead of building a great big student union that would blot out views from the college's hill, they would design a union as a three-level structure set into the hillside. His firm designed two-story dorms that wouldn't be too imposing (no high-rises here) and would blend with the rest of the college and the residential neighborhood.

Other ideas, including an amphitheater built into a hillside where the Hall of Science is now and a row of sorority, fraternity and other communal housing along Atherton Street, were never realized.

One idea Killingsworth and President Carl McIntosh championed that took root was tree planting. They believed trees would be aesthetically

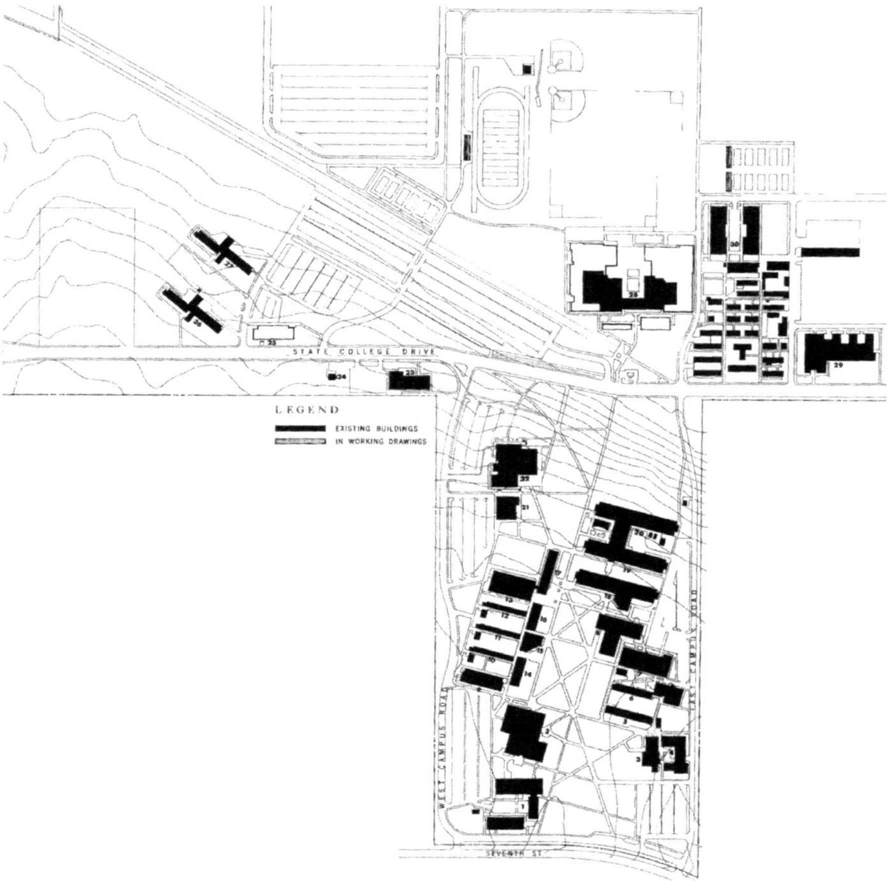

The campus as it looked in 1963. The two dorm buildings are on the left; the smaller temporary buildings are still in evidence on the upper right. The lower campus has a cafeteria but no student union yet. *Projected Master Plan for Long Beach State College.*

pleasing. Most importantly, according to several campus officials, the planting would obscure the monolithic concrete buildings already there.

As Jon Regnier, a student in the 1960s who went on to become associate vice-president for physical planning, put it, "He wanted to plant tons of trees to hide the ugly buildings."

Naturally, the State of California at the time would have frowned on a non-educational endeavor such as tree planting. So Killingsworth, with the enthusiastic backing of McIntosh and landscape architect Edward Lovell, took the issue to the community. They sought to raise $15,000 to buy three thousand of Helen Borcher's flowering peach trees with salmon-

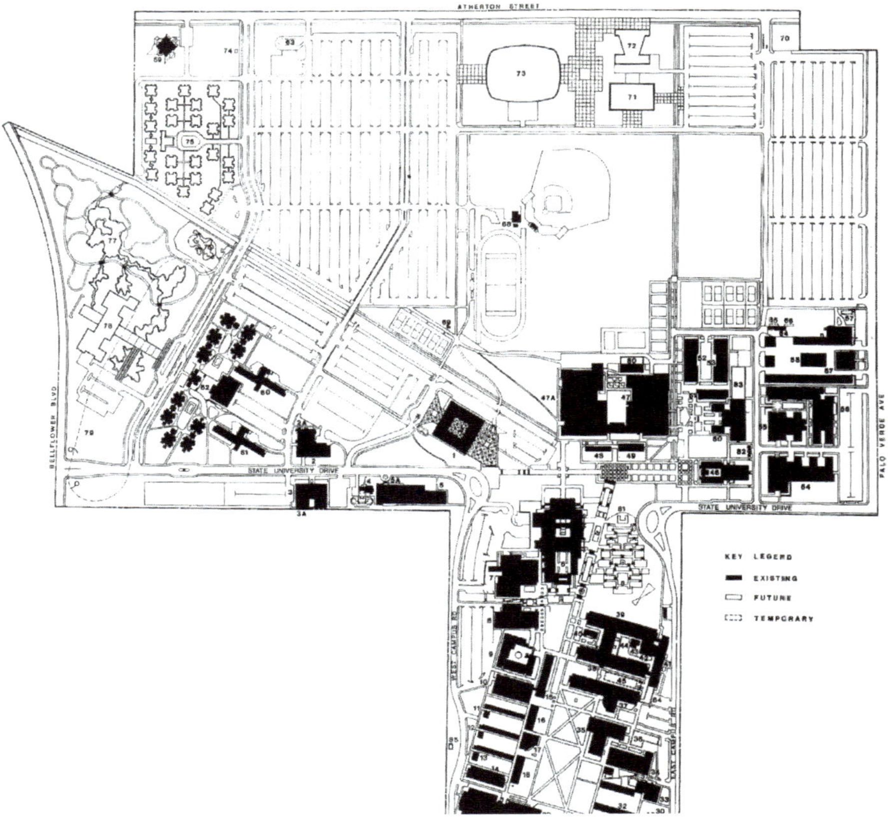

pink blossoms. The trees reminded everyone of the flowering cherry trees in Washington, D.C. Also, the small, bare-root trees were reasonably priced.

The idea was to generate donations from individuals as well as business leaders. They got money from the Long Beach Harbor commissioners; the United Nations Association of the United States of America, Long Beach Chapter; and Long Beach city employees, who contributed $857.

The Flowering Tree Committee of local leaders included Long Beach *Press-Telegram* newspaper editor and columnist Malcolm "Mac" Epley, who gave frequent updates on the campaign in his newspaper column "Beachcombing with Malcolm Epley." He included this item in his November 4, 1965 column: "The Sequoia Tribe of the Los Altos YMCA Indian Guides…voted to give $5 out of their precious wampum to help buy one of the 3,000 trees planned for the tree planting program." Epley offered Rose Bowl tickets for the winning tree-funding slogan. Some of the finalists included "Join the Peach Corps," "Empty Your Breeches to Plant Peaches" and "Practice What You Peach."

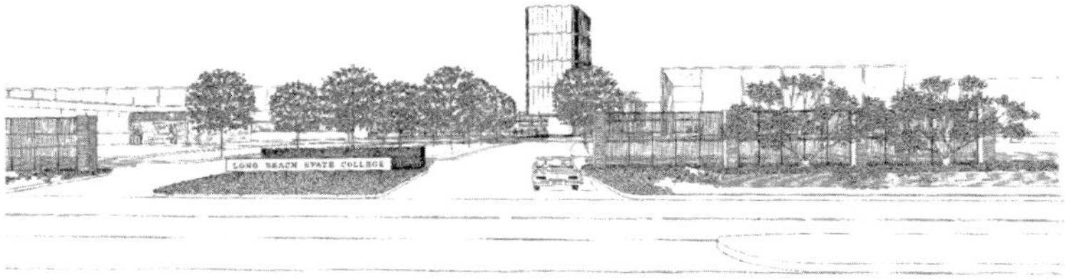

MASTER PLAN FOR LONG BEACH STATE COLLEGE

This new master plan for the Long Beach State College was developed under the necessity to accommodate an anticipated student body four times the 5,000 originally planned for ten years ago. It is part of a new design program instituted by the Trustees of the California State Colleges in which consulting architects will be selected to re-examine state college campuses in order to make changes necessary to handle California's swelling college population.

The architects here were asked to plan campus housing for 5,000, parking for 10,000 and educational and allied college facilities for a student body of 20,000. Half of the permanent buildings had already been constructed.

The site is 320 acres shaped in the form of a "T", the leg of which is 40 feet higher at its base than the rest of the campus. On the higher portion, the academic core was developed, thus limiting the expansion of this area. This drawback is symptomatic of the architectural problem of the school which was brought rapidly into existence without a sensitive relation of buildings, resulting in an unfortunate institutional anonymity for the existing campus.

Throughout the analysis and replanning of the campus the architects have tried to recognize the fine features of the original college and to develop these with the new so that the completed project will have the appearance of a total building program rather than one of parts. To correct the lack of architectural continuity, a new Central Entrance has been developed as a primary approach to the campus. This provides direct access to the Administrative Complex, the new Loop Drive, and the new Plaza. The entrance is wide with masonry pylons and on direct axis with a new nine-story office building which is developed as the theme structure of the campus. This building is located in the Plaza at the end of the tree-lined Loop Drive.

A complex traffic pattern for pedestrians, bicycles, and the auto-

(Continued on page 31)

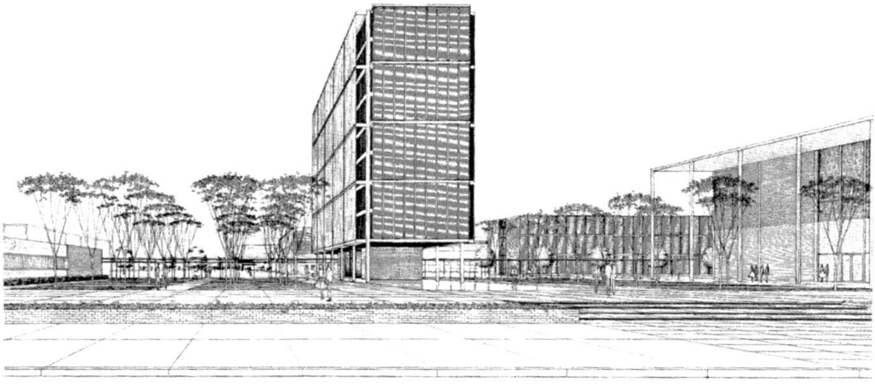

Above: The 1963 architect's plan included dorms and a nine-story structure that would become the McIntosh building. The campus's T-shape and rapid growth posed a planning challenge. *Courtesy of Physical Planning and Facilities Management.*

Opposite: By 1978, architects were sketching out plans for a music building (upper right), which would become the Carpenter Center; an assembly building next to it, which would become the Pyramid; and a Japanese Garden (upper left). All of those came to pass; a planned museum and arboretum on the western edge of campus did not. *Courtesy of Physical Planning and Facilities Management.*

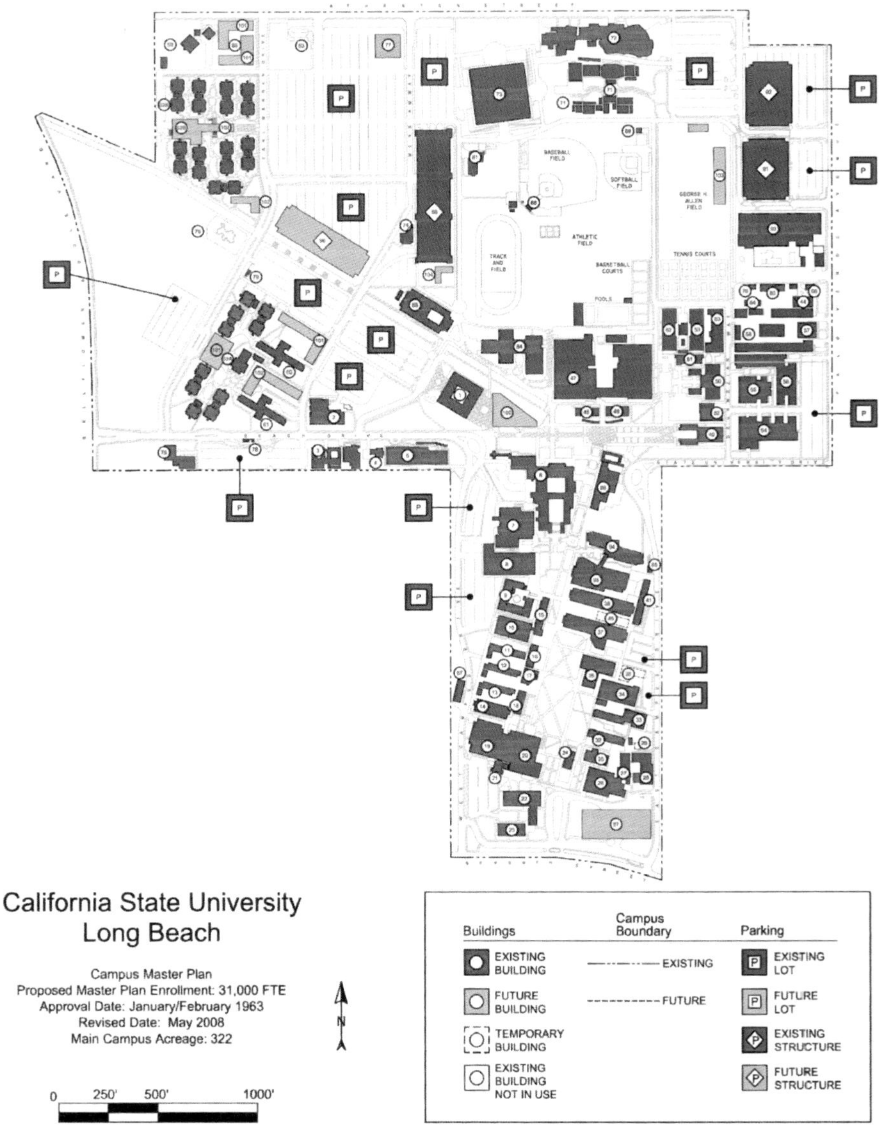

The 2008 campus master plan, with yet-unbuilt parking structures to the north and to the south, to be constructed if and when the university can get the funding to build them. *Courtesy of Physical Planning and Facilities Management.*

It didn't all go smoothly—fundraising took years, and supporters were forced to hurriedly raise money after the peach trees were purchased. But they got their peach trees, as well as ficus and Eucalyptus trees that eventually helped soften views of the unprepossessing structures.

Sculpture Symposium

The 1965 California International Sculpture Symposium was an audacious undertaking for the sixteen-year-old college.

Sculpture professor Kenneth Glenn, with the enthusiastic backing of Killingsworth and President Carl McIntosh, invited top artists from around the world to design giant sculptures that would be placed throughout the bare, underused and mostly treeless expanse. Nothing like it had been done before in the United States or on a college campus.

Then, everything went wrong. The summer symposium took longer than expected and cost more than anticipated. One commissioned sculptor got in a car accident with a state car he wasn't supposed to be driving, and another, frustrated he couldn't get the promised bronze cast for his work, dropped out in a huff. Others were disappointed with the Spartan dormitory accommodations. (The symposium was supposed to pay the artists' living expenses, and one artist brought both his wife and his mistress along.) Sculptors were seething and about to bolt.

That's when President Carl McIntosh called Hal Lynch, assistant dean of development, and told him he had a problem. McIntosh told the soft-spoken Lynch that he needed to step in to quiet an artist insurrection that was threatening the whole artistic dream.

"There was no money, people were irate and threatening to leave," recalled Lynch. "He said if we lose this, it will be the biggest embarrassment to the college." Lynch pulled out his own credit card to get artists their promised transportation and housing and just crossed his fingers until the bill came. Glenn "really tried to get things going, and he was able to reach out to these people with the state behind him," Lynch recalled. "But California couldn't get any money, the college couldn't get any money" and Glenn couldn't get enough financial backing.

"They really bit off more than they could chew," said University Art Museum interim director Brian Trimble, who noted that Glenn and crew originally planned to host exhibitions every five years and cover the city of Long Beach with as many as seventy public sculptures.

That didn't happen, but the symposium generated nine sculptures that still dot the campus, including one by Claire Falkenstein, who was a last-minute replacement for the Italian artist who got in a car wreck. Her thicket of welded metal was called *U as a Set* and occupies a fountain by the McIntosh building on upper campus.

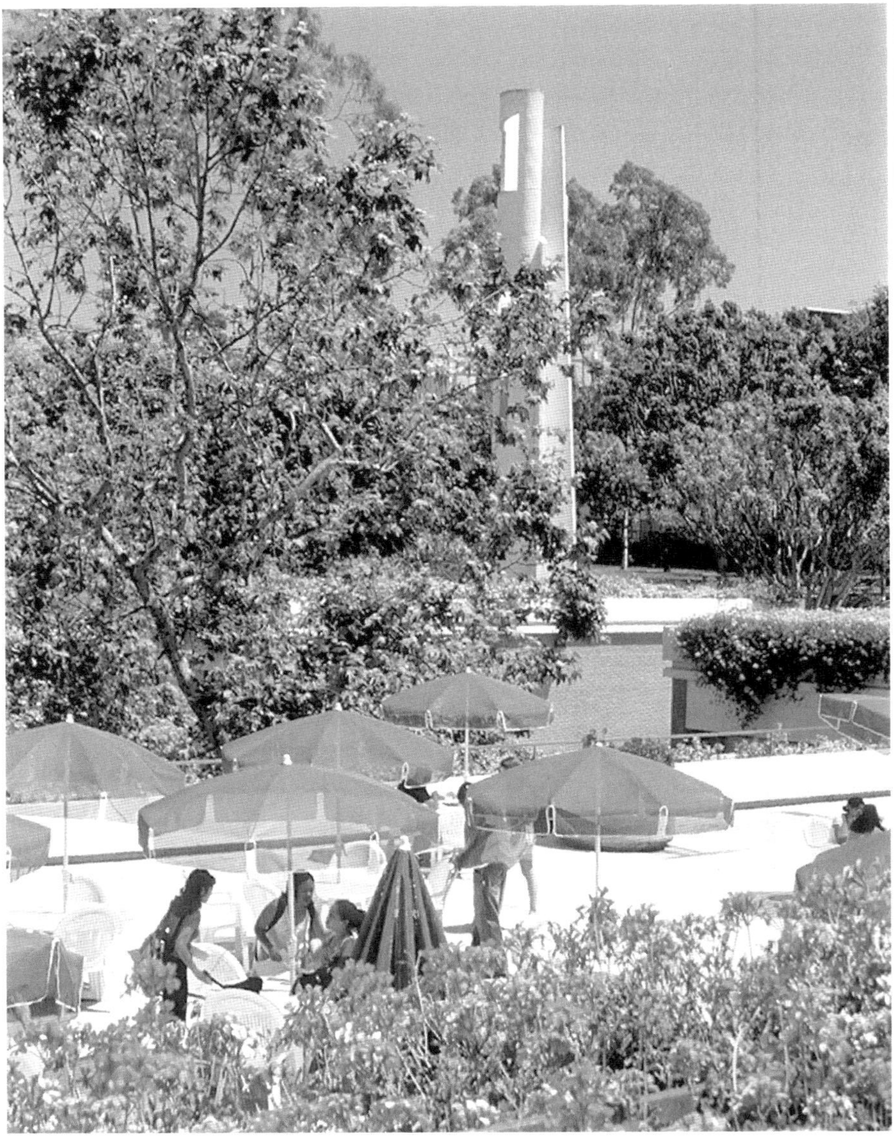

The Carson/Bloc bell tower, designed during the 1965 Sculpture Symposium, was finished in 1972. *Courtesy of the University Archives.*

The show was a campus-wide effort, and the enthusiasm eventually rubbed off on the skeptical community. Art students and professors scrounged everywhere for materials. Workers from the Long Beach Naval Shipyard finished some of the metal work. Then, as the structures started going up, residents got behind the project. The *Long Beach Press-Telegram* started writing stories. NBC's Marc Breslow, who later went on to *Price Is Right* fame, did a half-hour TV special on the symposium.

The pieces included an *Homage to Simon Rodia*, the creator of Watts Towers, who had died shortly before. Perhaps the best known of the pieces is *Now*, a sculpture by Piotr Kowalski. The sculpture, which resembles metallic, half-submerged tulip leaves, was created by exploding dynamite charges, attached to steel sheets, under water. North American Aviation in El Toro, California, subsidized the sculpture, and the company used Kowalski's work to further its research. Some of the metal extensions had to be replaced because students swung on them and broke them off.

Today, thousands of students tromp by *Now* on their way to class and the Coffee Bean and Tea Leaf nearby. The sculptures have become an accepted part of the campus hardscape. But in the mid-1960s, the work was unusual...and controversial. "You have to imagine the bulk of sculptures

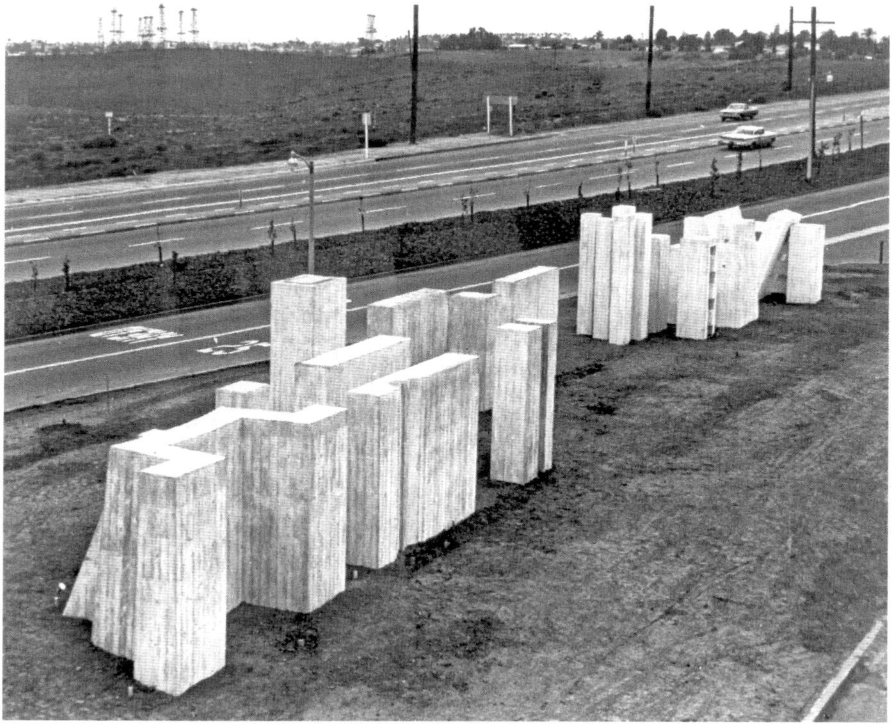

The sculpture *Homage to Simon Rodia* (the builder of the Watts Towers), by J.J. Beljon, is still a feature of the southern entrance. Rodia died shortly before the 1965 symposium started. Seventh Street is in the background of this mid-'60s view. *Courtesy of the University Archives.*

were up on this hill," said Trimble, as he prepared for a fiftieth-anniversary celebration of the exhibit. "It wasn't until later that the student union and other buildings were built. You literally entered the campus into this sculpture park. "There were some who loved it and also those on campus and in the community who just didn't get it."

There are now twenty-one public sculptures on the campus, including one work that sculpture students started in 1965 with leftover timbers from other projects. The students fashioned them into a fifteen-ton, twelve-foot-high and forty-four-foot-long work that resembles large railroad ties tossed helter skelter into an enormous pile. Their *Homage to Kenn Glenn* still sits up near the campus entrance on Seventh Street—a public acknowledgement to the wildly ambitious, one-of-a-kind exhibit that is now part of the campus landscape.

THE JAPANESE GARDEN

In the mid-1970s, Loraine Miller Collins wanted to donate $250,000 to honor her late husband, Earl Burns Miller, with a garden at the new Long Beach Art Museum, which was to be built downtown. Who would design it? None other than architectural luminary I.M. Pei, who would go on to design the John F. Kennedy Library in Boston and the grand Louvre Pyramid in Paris. In the 1970s, Pei drew up plans for a garden at a new Long Beach art museum to be built near city hall.

There was only one problem: Miller Collins, who had by this time remarried, didn't like the plans she saw. So she showed them to her longtime friend Ed Lovell, the landscape architect at Long Beach State. Lovell, a veteran whose father had designed one of the first houses on Park Avenue in Belmont Shore, wasn't impressed either. He spoke with the city manager. He told the official, "If this is I.M. Pei's idea of a garden, he should stick to his architecture and not be designing gardens." He thought the garden was too urban, too crowded, too much like an amusement park and nothing like the sanctuary Earl Burns Miller would have wanted. That was his opinion, anyway, and Collins apparently agreed.

Lovell said he helped Collins get her $250,000 back and then started working on plans for a garden on the Long Beach State campus. Collins called Lovell up with the idea of building a Japanese garden, and he agreed.

Planning was held up for two years when Collins's husband, Larry Collins, told her that building a garden during a drought was a bad idea.

The drought ended, and work proceeded in 1980. Lovell and Collins visited Japan several times, and Lovell took hundreds of photos, trying to capture the aesthetic of gardens in Japan. Lovell read every book on Japanese gardens he could find. His plans included pine trees and bamboo plants and incorporated greenery that would flourish in the Long Beach climate. He added a teahouse and a bridge. Lovell said the teahouse rests at a higher elevation than the rest of the garden, symbolizing the elevation distinction between the forest and the mountains.

When it opened in 1981, some students and others protested that the garden wasn't a true Japanese garden and that more Japanese students and faculty should have been consulted. One student took issue with the fact that concrete boulders were used instead of real ones. Lovell replied that the money ran out and concrete boulders would just have to do.

The garden, built on 1.3 acres between the dorms and a sea of lower campus parking lots, was to be a place where people could walk over the bridge and see the teahouse, the bamboo and bonsai and hear nothing but the bubbling stream below. "We wanted a place where people could get away and be alone with nature…where you could go and forget your

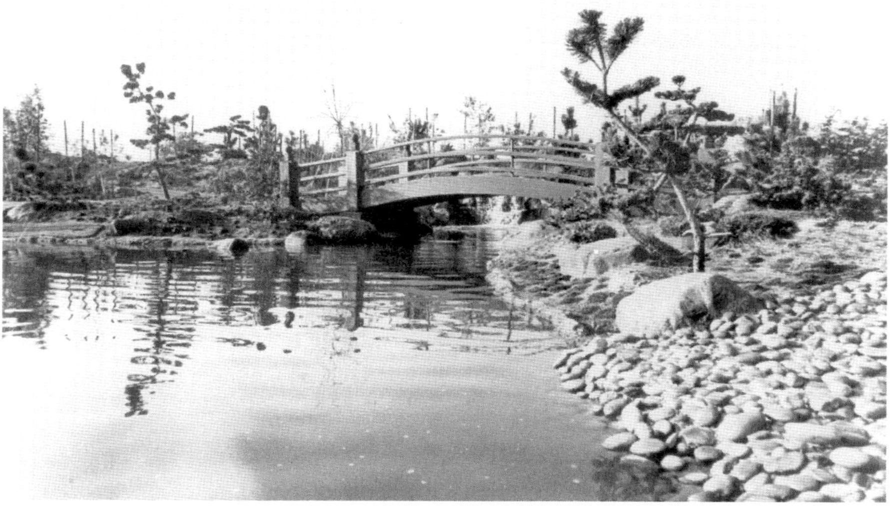

The Japanese Garden in the early 1980s, when the trees were still small. *Courtesy of the University Archives.*

cares of the world," he said. "People came up and told me, 'It worked, you know.'"

Through the 1960s, '70s and '80s, the campus started to bloom with small trees, larger-than-life sculptures and concrete-and-brick buildings going up at an impressive pace. But according to the college's longest-serving president, some of those much-needed buildings were going up in the wrong places. The campus aesthetics were actually the least controversial of the issues that landed on the desk of Stephen Horn.

6

Seventeen Years with Stephen Horn

"They Thought He Was Nuts"

John Stephen "Steve" Horn, the Stanford- and Harvard-educated son of a bacteriologist-chemist father and a pulp-fiction writer mother, said he was always encouraged to give his opinion—on the Roosevelt administration, World War II, Communism, you name it.

"Not being a bashful little boy…I had plenty to say on the subject," he said. And he had a lot to say about the layout of the Long Beach State campus. One of his first acts was to order administrators to stop "cluttering" up the campus with concrete buildings. He told one dean that he "did not want another tree cut down without the issue coming to me for a decision." He said the proposed location of one building on upper campus was "simply unbelievable" and ordered it moved, according to an unpublished campus history.

The campus is like a T, with a big fat top and a skinny stem. For years, virtually all the buildings were constructed on the skinny stem toward the south, which was considered the campus's main street. Officials in the early days couldn't fathom needing all that space to the north and stuck to that idea, even during the 1960s, when the school ballooned from ten thousand students in 1960 to twenty-six thousand by 1970.

When Long Beach State started with 322 acres, it enjoyed a wealth of acreage compared with some other campuses. Cal State Fullerton, for instance, has 236 acres; the University of Southern California has 226. The first president, P. Victor Peterson, revealed years later that he and campus officials would spitball about what to do with the northern part of

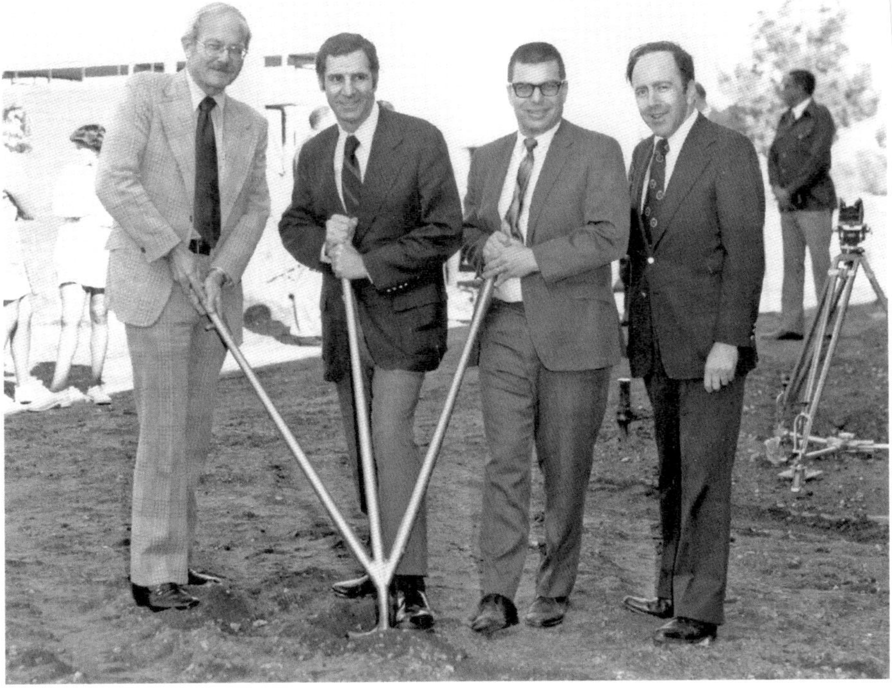

Breaking ground on the addition to the health services building in 1975, one of many construction projects completed during the Horn era. *Left to right*: architect Kenny Wing Jr., state senator George Deukmejian, director of physical planning and development Jon Regnier and President Steve Horn. *Courtesy of the University Archives.*

campus. Agriculture? Farming? Parking? Sports? They used much of it for parking and recreation, and the rest they left to the sheep and the rabbits.

As the student population exploded beyond anyone's imagination, planners were forced to regroup. But the library and all the main buildings stayed at one edge of the campus, with parking and physical education to the north on lower campus. The 1963 master plan said it was pretty much too late to do anything about it.

Campus planners tried to make it work, but when the new president, Stephen Horn, saw plans in 1970 to build another liberal arts building in the central quad, an area that was finally getting a little more attractive with trees and sculptures, he demanded it be moved. He essentially tossed it down the hill to start the state approval process over again. That's when legislators decided Dominguez Hills needed the building more than Long Beach State

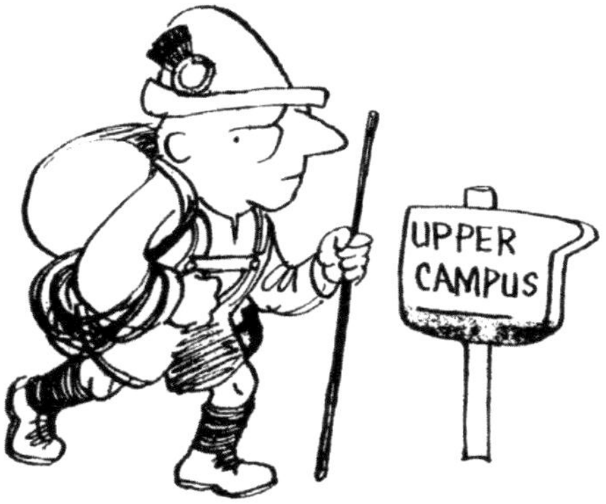

Students and faculty complained that parking was on one end of the campus, while almost all of the buildings were on another. It was an issue that particularly irked Steve Horn. *Courtesy of the* Forty-Niner.

did, and they gave it to the smaller college up the 405 Freeway. Horn had to lobby legislators to get funding to build another one.

Today, the social science/ public affairs building sits in the campus flatlands to the north next to the engineering building. Horn did the same thing with Brotman Hall, the administration building, which now occupies the dusty space once used for the Forty-Niner Days celebration.

Former dean Francis "Frenchy" Flynn admitted to Horn later that he thought Horn was nuts to put those buildings where he did. Horn just laughed. He never had a problem doing things his own way. He was born in Gilroy in 1931 and raised in San Juan Bautista in a family that was not poor but lived a country existence. There was no electricity until Stephen was ten and no telephone until he was a high school senior. Young Horn climbed the oil rigs that were rising up in the farming community in the 1940s. His keen interest in government would bookend his time at Cal State Long Beach from 1970 to 1988.

He worked as an administrative assistant for the U.S. secretary of labor and a U.S. senator in the years before he came to Long Beach State and was a Republican U.S. congressman after he left the college. He was also vice-chairman of the U.S. Civil Rights Commission.

Scott Charmack, who was a deputy with campus physical planning and facilities management, recalls that, once, the president abruptly asked him to lunch to discuss personnel issues. Charmack was taken aback at the president's invitation but relieved that he happened to be wearing his sports jacket. Horn fired questions, demanded to know every single detail and took copious notes. By the end, Charmack had broken into a cold sweat. "That jacket was soaking wet," he recalled.

At the university, Horn had plenty to say about a lot of things, and sometimes he would follow up with decisive—some faculty would say "dictatorial"—action. In 1973, Horn clashed with popular and winning basketball coach Jerry Tarkanian after an NCAA investigation led to allegations of recruiting violations and special treatment for players.

Tarkanian soon left—his family members maintain he simply found a better job at UNLV, but Horn said in an oral interview that he had personally fired the coach.

Horn previously had little interest in sports, or in exercise for that matter. He said his drive to clean up the Long Beach State basketball and football programs came after a chance dinner chat with legendary UCLA basketball coach John Wooden. The coach, according to Horn, mentioned that Long Beach State was not part of the national letter of intent program, which is designed to prevent schools from stealing other team's players. Wooden used the words "bandit operation" in reference to Long Beach State. This raised Horn's hackles and prompted him to take an interest in athletics and, eventually, in the powerful National Collegiate Athletic Association.

Horn started attending NCAA meetings in the Midwest, one of the first university presidents to do so. The NCAA members were tickled at first. By the mid-1970s, Horn had grown keenly aware that his own university's athletic program was deeply in debt, due to hefty fines imposed by the NCAA, and only playing before modest crowds. He proposed that the NCAA member schools share TV revenue with the poorer schools such as his own. It was like a bomb went off at the 1975 convention. He was labeled "Robin Hood." USC football coach John McKay seethed, saying Horn's plan amounted to communism and asked, according to the *Independent Press-Telegram*, "Where did he come from anyway?"

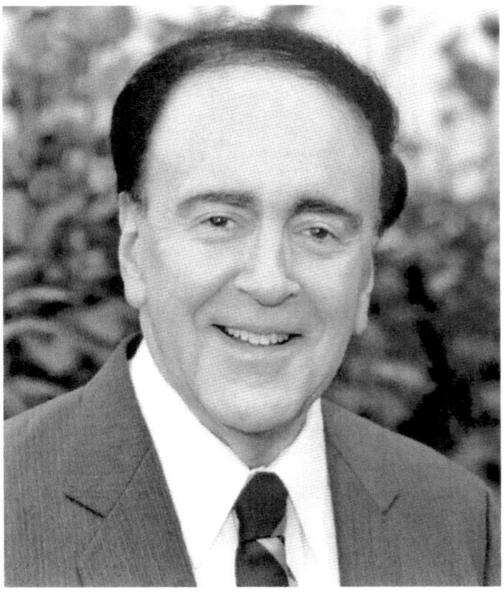

Steve Horn, who was president for seventeen and a half years before getting elected to Congress, frequently feuded with faculty. Still, he presided over a period of expansion that saw the college grow into a university. *Courtesy of CSULB.*

Horn, meanwhile, had launched a letter-writing campaign to get all member presidents involved in the NCAA, and Horn's lobbed grenade got the college presidents' attention. A president's commission was formed. Before, athletic directors had gotten involved in the NCAA, not presidents. The commission was quickly wooed by the rich schools—a turn of events Horn hadn't planned on. There were lawsuits, and groups within the NCAA splintered off.

To make a very long story short, TV revenue is now shared among conference members and, to an extent, within the NCAA. "All those things he promoted came to pass," said Perry Moore, the athletic director Horn hired to take charge of the athletic program after NCAA sanctions were imposed. But at the time, "they thought he was nuts."

Long Beach was reeling from NCAA four-year sanctions in basketball and football and the $400,000 fine levied by the NCAA. Horn talked of dropping the football program. But that didn't happen, then at least. Moore got athletics more closely aligned with academics, partly by having coaches teach classes and getting them on the university payroll instead of the athletics budget. The university essentially kept the NCAA off its back for more than thirty years, until 2007, when the basketball program was sanctioned for bringing in ineligible junior college transfers.

Off the field at Long Beach State, classroom evaluations were being instituted and alumni fundraising efforts were becoming professionalized. Records were no longer kept in shoe boxes, and the alumni group went from what was, at times, a beer-swigging, strip club–visiting experience to a more professional organization. Change in alumni affairs started back in 1970, prompting the *Forty-Niner* headline, "CSULB Starts Keeping Records of Alumni Ater 20 Years of Not Doing It."

Horn bristled when a *Press-Telegram* columnist called Long Beach State the "hilltop mausoleum." The insult was meant for the perceived lack of student spirit at sporting events, but it also alluded to a lack of college involvement in the Greater Long Beach community. Horn and his wife, Nini, tried to combat that perception by getting more involved through social events and fundraisers. He got a state law changed to start affordable senior education on campus. He also launched a fundraising and arts initiative that, in later years, produced the Richard and Karen Carpenter Performing Arts Center and other endeavors intended to draw the community to campus. The Isabel Patterson Child Development Center also came into being during the Horn era, thanks to a donation from Patterson, one of the earliest students.

Horn also hired David Adamany as academic vice-president, and Adamany championed the idea that faculty should do research. But professors hired under the Peterson-era ethos that to publish is to perish (at Long Beach State) bristled, since they said little was being done to ease their four-class teaching load. Despite the protests, faculty were encouraged and expected to do more research along with teaching.

Horn clashed early and often with faculty, who found him arrogant and unwilling to listen to them and too willing to act unilaterally. They censured him twice. Emeritus history professor David Bernstein said Horn acted with hostility toward the tenure system, while other faculty complained he made them vulnerable to layoffs in the early '80s when the university faced severe budget cuts.

But Bernstein, who was a union leader, said the president could separate the personal from the professional. When a senior colleague tried to block Bernstein's promotion for political reasons, Horn wouldn't buy it. He said if the professor was teaching well, doing research and contributing to the university, then he should be promoted. "He wasn't interested in the petty politics," Bernstein said. "We had no relationship beyond that of a president and a critical faculty member, an active member of the union. We disagreed on almost everything, but he did not take it personally as far as I could tell."

However, clashes with faculty were taking their toll, and when Horn locked horns with Cal State chancellor W. Ann Reynolds, it was the beginning of the end. (Reynolds also clashed with other campus presidents and trustees and was herself forced out.) Horn resigned in 1988.

He taught a political science class and was given an office in the library, away from the rest of the faculty. Rosemary Taylor Schmidt, who was head of the alumni association, called Horn in his library office and got a voicemail saying students calling him should dial him up at home. And he left his number.

"He suffered quite a bit of embarrassment," said Taylor Schmidt, who added she got along with Horn, "working in the library and inviting students to call him at home to talk about class work."

Taylor Schmidt's husband, Ron Schmidt, a longtime political science faculty member and chair, recalls that Horn's style was confrontational and "very high-handed. That gave him more grief than he needed."

Politics, and the effects of his own rather forceful personality, may have ended his academic career, but he wasn't finished. He ran for Congress in 1988, losing to conservative Republican and 1969 Long Beach State grad Dana Rohrabacher. But Horn ran for a newly apportioned Thirty-eighth Congressional District in 1992 and won as a moderate Republican. He stayed for ten years, until another reapportionment by Democrats tilted his district to the other party.

Mark Mayuga, a 1969 design graduate who later worked at the university and was family friends with the Horns, said Horn "had a vision, and it was not some airy-fairy thing. He really had a vision of what Cal State Long Beach was and what the standards should be. A lot

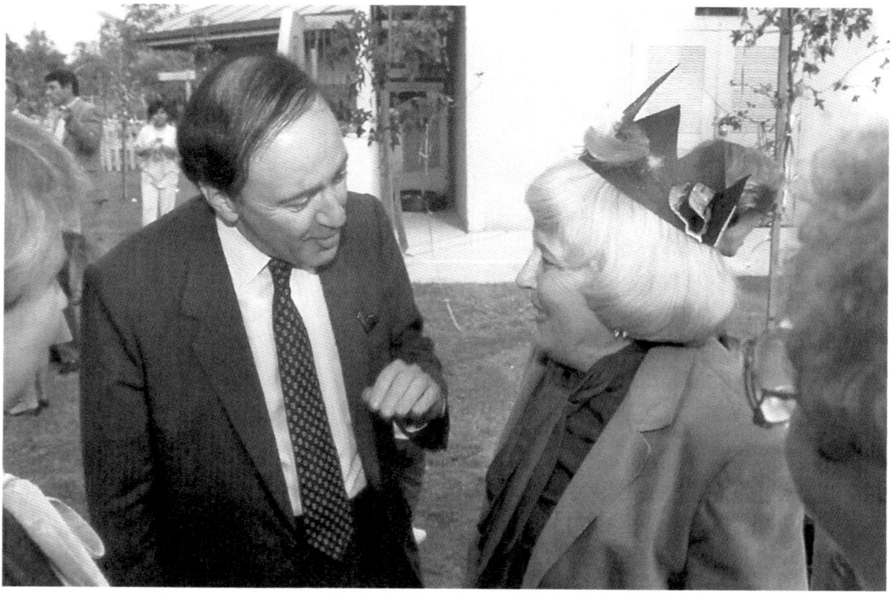

Steve Horn with Isabel Patterson, one of the first students at the college, whose donations made the Child Development Center possible. *Courtesy of the University Archives.*

of professors bucked it because it threatened their tenure. He tried to hold professors to a higher standard."

Horn retired in 2001 and died ten years later from complications from Alzheimer's disease. The university staged a celebration of his life, complete with PowerPoint presentations and testimonials describing the buildings he moved and the changes he made to Long Beach State during his seventeen years as president.

Ron Schmidt said Horn "had clear ideas about what he wanted, and he made it happen…Leaders bring people together to make things happen. He didn't necessarily bring people together, but he did have a good compass about what needed to be done."

7

Campus Life Is a-Changin'

"Those Were Goofy Times"

After Rosemary Taylor Schmidt graduated from Long Beach State in 1964, her alma mater hired her to work in student activities. Her first duty was to teach college women how to walk properly through a receiving line.

When she became pregnant with her first child, she had to get the president's approval to continue working. Even then, a memo went around warning Schmidt's co-workers in great detail about all the unpleasant physiological events that could happen to a pregnant woman late in her term. Just in case something, you know, happened. That was 1965. Three years later, she was giving campus police a friendly heads-up after a graduate student and his friends sprinkled the campus lawn with ten naked, full-sized plaster and wax statues, some engaged in pornographic acts involving TV sets. The event became a national incident, and a trial judge called the exhibit "an inch away from an act of perversion."

That was about the time some students and professors put on a performance of *Hair*, complete with the nude scene, in Lecture Hall 150 near the liberal arts buildings. "Those were goofy times," Taylor Schmidt later said.

Taylor Schmidt experienced the head-spinning era as campuses nationwide transitioned from relatively chaste and restricted in the 1950s to the freethinking and free-loving institutions of the 1960s. As a student, then activities director and later associate vice-president of student services, she had a front-row seat to the revolution.

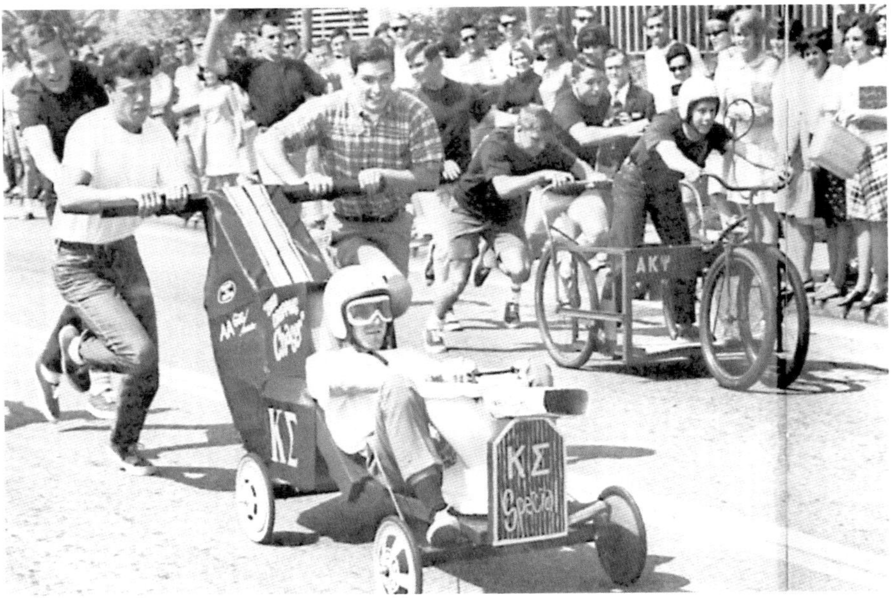

Fraternities race go-carts in the 1960s. Fraternities and sororities were the engines that drove campus life in the college's first decades. *Courtesy of CSULB.*

When she was a student, Taylor Schmidt and her female classmates wore dresses or skirts and blouses to class every day—capris and pants were only for finals week. Off-the-shoulder dresses, slacks or sundresses were taboo, according to the *Long Beach State Nugget Guide* to proper student behavior.

As for the men, they could forget about wearing Bermuda shorts or sporting facial hair and were reminded by the *Nugget* authors, "There probably is a place for sweat shirts and grease stained trousers—but it isn't on the LBSC campus."

The rules were just as clear for the few students living in student housing. The first dorms, Los Cerritos and Los Alamitos, opened in 1959, and students paid nineteen dollars a semester. After 10:00 p.m., no men could visit the women's dorms, and a "white-haired lady stood at the door" and made sure no one went in, recalled 1962 graduate Bill Tilney. He also remembered watching the Kennedy-Nixon debates in glorious black and white in the dorm lounge in 1960.

Tilney, who was student body president, planned to drop out after his father died his senior year. But Lois Swanson, the associate dean of student affairs, and Dean Francis Flynn came up with $300 to help make ends meet,

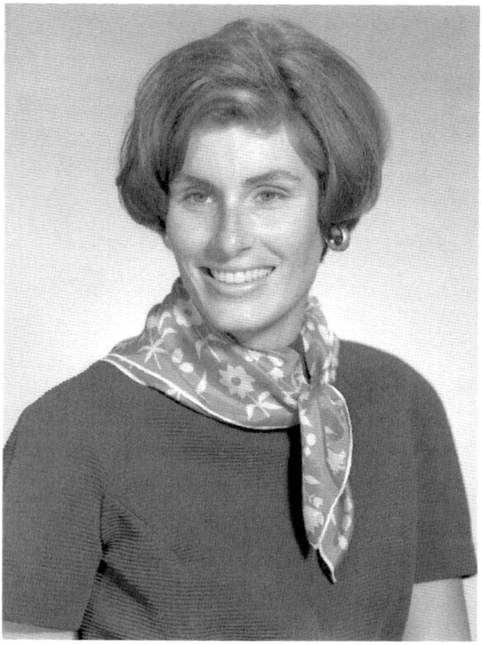

Left: Student Rosemary Taylor Schmidt was a saloon girl at Forty-Niner Days in the early 1960s and became activities director in the late 1960s when campus life got interesting. *Courtesy of the University Archives.*

Below: Los Cerritos and Los Alamitos opened in 1959. After 10:00 p.m., no men could visit the women's dorms, and a "white-haired lady stood at the door" and made sure no one went in, recalls 1962 graduate Bill Tilney. *Courtesy of CSULB.*

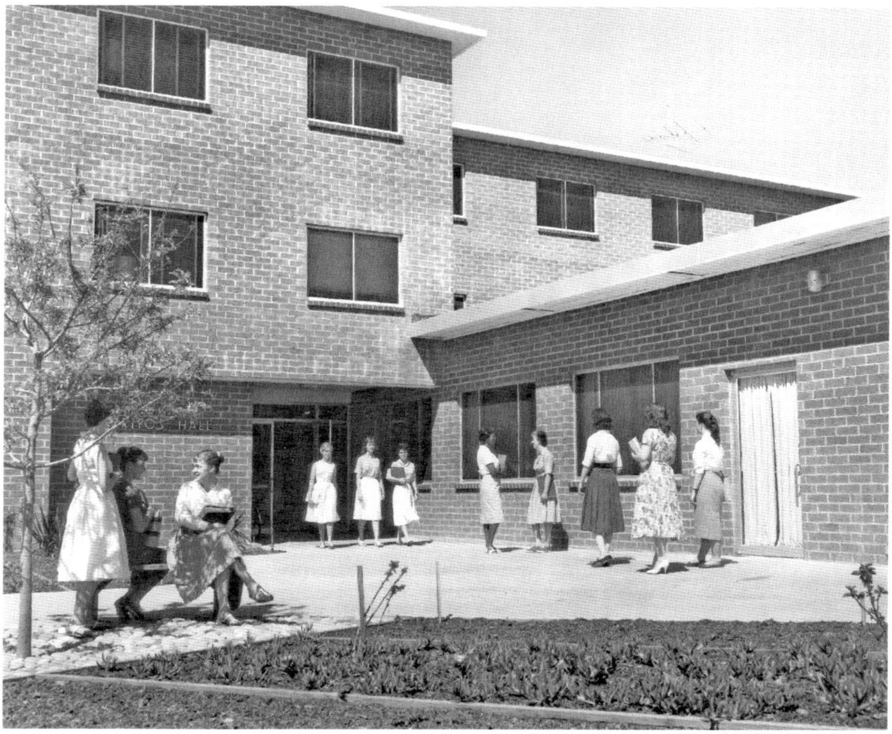

which "made a huge difference." He became one of the first Peace Corps volunteers in Ethiopia and, later, mayor of El Paso, Texas.

Tilney, whose father was from Scotland and mother was from Mexico, remembers a friendly campus and a mostly white student body. But that was changing.

Schmidt, a member of the homecoming court, said she "pranced around as a dance hall girl" at Forty-Niner Days, the annual event that honored the heady, occasionally barbaric, times of the gold rush that gave the campus its mascot and nickname. As the years rolled by, she came to view the annual rite differently.

The annual festival, which took place on lower campus near where Brotman Hall is now, was the uniting campus social event. The idea was to reenact the frenetic hurly-burly of that era and, by extension, the circus-comes-to-town founding of Long Beach State one hundred years later.

Revelers labored all night, constructing prefabricated saloons and other gold rush–era buildings. Young men shouted impatient, last-minute instructions in the darkness, carrying a bottle of beer in one hand and a can of creosote, the carcinogenic substance made to age wood, in another. Some of the saloons and other buildings constructed for the event were later used at Knott's Berry Farm.

At noon the next day, a crowd gathered with Nugget, the donkey mascot, in tow. The honorary sheriff cut the ribbon, the crowd waded in and Forty-Niner Days commenced. It was a lot of fun, a little dangerous at times and also eye-poppingly insensitive by today's standards.

"People would dress up like drunk Mexicans leaning on posts or Chinese coolies with laundry," Taylor Schmidt recalls. "There were representations of American Indians as stereotypical playthings...we did not have the essence to understand what that was all about."

Taylor Schmidt looks back at those days feeling "stultifyingly stupid about the world. I didn't know what was going on then. I didn't know about hunger. Then, you didn't think about your place in the world. The '50s were like that."

But Taylor Schmidt and some of her friends could feel "a slow rebellion" brewing. She worked for the popular Lois Swanson, the associate dean of student affairs from 1951 to 1970, who was instrumental in setting up the Greek system on campus, the student government, a host of activities and even the University Student Union.

The Greek system came under fire in the late 1960s. Some sororities on campus were banned from recognition after officials learned that they weren't

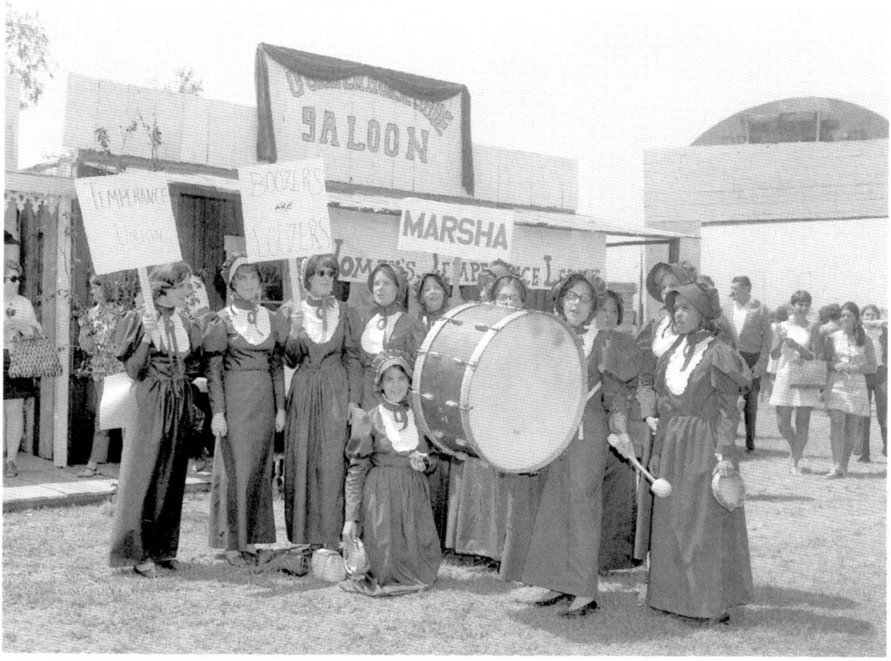

Forty-Niner Days, 1960s version. Students made costumes and constructed buildings from the period, the best of which were later carted off to Knott's Berry Farm for use at the amusement park. *Courtesy of the University Archives.*

allowed to select their own members. The national leaders were requiring photos of women pledging to local chapters, Taylor Schmidt recalled. It had to do with race—the campus chapters wanted to admit black women, but certain national chapters wouldn't allow it. Swanson effectively banned the sororities until the local chapters were permitted to select their own members. "The whole thing was miserable for everyone," recalled Taylor Schmidt.

In 1962, student body president Gary Little sent a telegram to James Meredith, the African American student barred from Ole Miss. Meredith wanted to study law. "We the Associated Students of Long Beach State College would be proud to have you as a member of our student body," Little wrote. "We deplore the treatment afforded you there." The overture was reported in the *Long Beach Independent* newspaper. "It was absurd on the face of it because we don't have a law school," Little said later. But several students wanted to make the gesture. They got a mixed reaction, with younger students supporting it and others not so sure. Students and faculty were also discovering that prejudice sometimes started at home.

Several years later, the *Forty-Niner* investigated a new African American professor's fruitless quest to find a landlord who would rent an apartment to her in Long Beach.

On campus, students started to demand classes more relevant to an increasingly diverse student body. Black and Chicano studies came into being in the late 1960s. Women's studies began about 1970, and some classes drew the ire of conservatives later on when classes in women's self-examination were being taught, complete with slides and models.

The popular Forty-Niner Days, increasingly seen as somewhat silly or downright offensive, faced boycotts from some student groups. With the Vietnam conflict escalating, students were watching their friends ship off to Southeast Asia, aware that they could be next. They started protesting the war and questioning administrators who seemed to promote what they considered antiquated, even oppressive notions of conduct and morality.

By 1968, headlines had started appearing in the *Forty-Niner* such as "Black Student Union Holds Senate Hostage" and "Joan Baez and Husband Come to Campus to Discourage…Draft" and "Fist Fights Plague Demonstration" over military recruiting on campus. Tuition worries flared as "5,000 from campus community gather in the central quad to hear students and faculty lash out at [California governor Ronald] Reagan for proposing tuition requirement."

One art exhibit by a graduate art student ignited some of the fiercest protests of all. Bill Spater produced ten larger-than-life statues depicting what he called in his 1968 thesis "the absurdity of our contemporary minds." He portrayed women straddling baby carriages and ironing boards. Some figures were having intimate relations with television sets. (One can only wonder what the artist could have done with smart phones and iPads.) The figures were visually arresting and rarely clothed.

Spater was required to have the work displayed in order to get his degree. Campus officials dithered about displaying the work before finally saying no. They still awarded Spater his degree, but the work had not been shown as was customary for master's students.

At 7:00 a.m. on April Fool's Day 1968, Spater got his show—on the main campus lawn. Spater and his friends had dragged the statues out from the art room, roped them off and stood guard. A little later, Rosemary Taylor Schmidt's phone rang.

"I scurried over to the grass out in front of the Art Department," she recalled. "I walk up there, and there was this life-size figure. There was a TV there, and there was a guy's face inside the TV. There was a [statue of a] grown person standing outside the TV" with what might be called an essential body part inside. There were other such statues, and they were all over the grass. "It was very creative—kind of before its time."

A crowd of students formed, and city residents joined the throng, until there were about two thousand in all. The police came, and by midmorning, the show was over. The sculptures were removed from the lawn on orders from President Carl McIntosh.

Students claimed this was artist censorship. They posted photos of the statues on bulletin boards on campus. The campus police chief took them down. Professors posted photos of the statues in the same places. The police chief took them down, too. There were protests and demonstrations. A restricted, eighteen-and-over showing was scheduled for May.

But Cal State chancellor Glenn Dumke cancelled the exhibit, and California governor Reagan backed him, and the *Forty-Niner* quoted him as saying there was no need for "pornography" on campus. The move led to massive protests, a large police response and forty-three arrests, one being a professor. The *Forty-Niner* claimed it was the first time students were arrested for civil disobedience in the twenty-one-year history of the campus.

The actions led to lawsuits and more protests, but in the end, the guerrilla art show on the campus lawn was the only mass viewing Spater got for his work. Some campus professors did create a modest little showing by buying Spater's statues for one cent and displaying them in their offices. The Academic Senate censured Dumke, and students contributed bail money for the jailed students. Summer break came, and students scattered.

Still, Long Beach State didn't see the violence that other campuses experienced in the '60s. And things weren't always so serious. One professor, Peter Silverman, made arrangements for a camel to be ridden across campus. Another time, he reclined on the grass on upper campus and had himself covered in spaghetti.

Taylor Schmidt recalls watching Joan Baez and Jefferson Airplane performing on Hardfact Hill by the science building. She escorted an exhausted Angela Davis to a speaking event but not before encouraging the well-known activist to nap in her office. One weekend, The Doors played at the Gold Mine gym, and people complained because students climbed over the bushes to get into the cramped space.

Taylor Schmidt retired from the campus in 2000 after thirty-five years. Like a lot of people who worked with students, she learned to take things as they come. "It was a very conservative campus. It wasn't a campus out of L.A., like UCLA," Taylor Schmidt said. "But it did have its spunk."

BILL SPATER

Accidental Careers, Academic and Otherwise

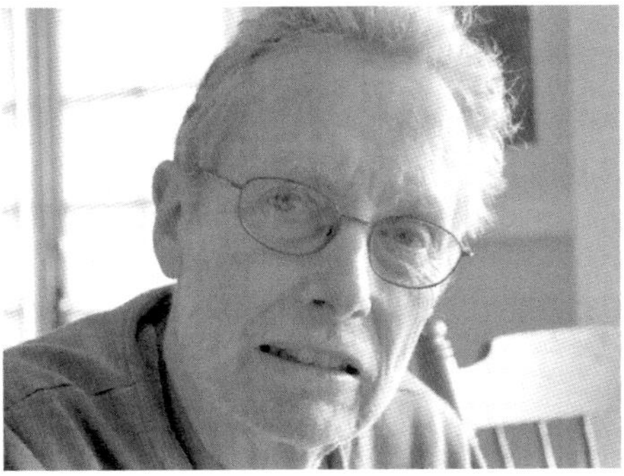

Bill Spater, who works as a lawyer helping the poor and indigent appeal their cases, said he didn't mean to launch a revolution. He said he was tired of the indecision over whether his nude sculptures would be shown, so he showed them himself. *Courtesy of Bill Spater.*

Sculpture artist Bill Spater hadn't intended to create pornography for his graduate thesis. He also hadn't intended to have a career in law. But those things came together, happily for him.

The Inglewood resident said he worked for two and a half years on his controversial sculptures. The work contained a touch of mid-century fantasy—a Venus rising from an ironing board and another woman with cowboy boots straddling an ironing board.

He said he wanted to be provocative. "I thought I was making something that would promote dialogue...something that was thought-provoking, not cheap or lurid. I was serious about it. As serious as a college student could be."

When the chancellor's quashing of a public exhibit spurred arrests and police in riot gear milling near Seventh Street, Spater decided things were "way, way out of control. Considering the danger we presented as students, it was an overreaction." He contends the protests would have blown over had the chancellor just allowed the exhibit behind closed doors.

Spater sued. The American Civil Liberties Union represented him, and that's when he met the legendary ACLU attorney Fred Okrand. He spent hours in the court hallways chatting with Okrand, who once represented Japanese citizens forced into internment camps and teachers forced to take loyalty oaths. Those idle hours spent talking about civil rights, freedom of speech and other issues made an impression on young Spater. Okrand became a mentor.

After grad school, Spater was drafted and decided to seek conscientious objector status. He entered social work and discovered he was good at it. Then, he thought about his conversations with Okrand and applied to law school.

Spater is now a staff attorney with the California Appellate Project in Los Angeles, where he helps convicted indigent and juveniles appeal their cases. He and other attorneys research the cases and help the defendants find a qualified lawyer.

The plaster and wax statues he created in 1968 were plaster casts meant to be gilded in bronze. That never happened, and the statues deteriorated. But Spater's thesis, *The Wonderful World of Plaster and Wax*, can now be found at the campus library. The "restricted circulation" warning has been crossed out in red.

8

The Tarkanian Years and the Gold Mine Gym

"Hotter Than Hot, Louder Than Loud"

In the late 1960s, Long Beach State didn't have a fancy gym, a beautiful campus or a high-powered program to draw recruits to its modest basketball team.

True, the team was coached by a young Jerry Tarkanian, who had come from Pasadena City College. That was before Tarkanian became famous for leading the Runnin' Rebels to a national championship, drawing the full attention of the NCAA infractions department in the process.

But that's not what registered with top recruit Glenn McDonald, a six-foot, six-inch forward. What convinced him, in 1970, to pass up USC, Pepperdine, Arizona, Arizona State and several other schools and come to Long Beach State was the Soul Squad. "The thing that really got me was we had black cheerleaders," said McDonald. "They had regular cheerleaders, white ones here and black cheerleaders over here. I was intrigued because I never saw that at any other school. It was one of the big reasons I came to this school."

McDonald said he didn't have plans to date members of the Soul Squad. He just thought it was kind of cool that the college had a black cheerleading squad and that fans seemed to enjoy cheering with them.

The Soul Squad lasted only a few years, and the men's basketball program's days in the national limelight lasted just a little longer, from 1968 to 1974.

McDonald hit that sweet spot between two coaching legends. He played for Tarkanian from 1971 to '73 and then one year for future Basketball-

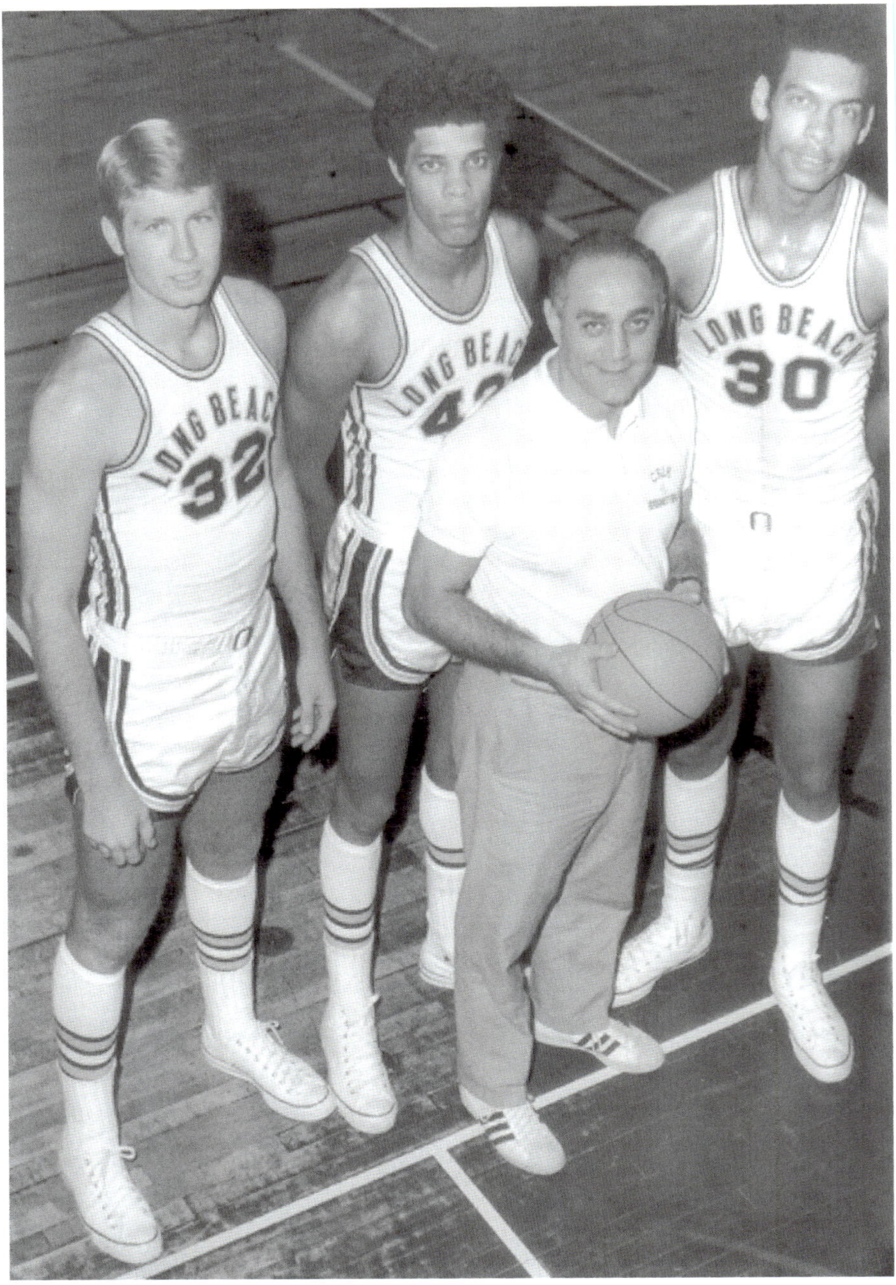

Former 49er basketball coach Jerry Tarkanian with three of his stars. *Left to right*: Chuck Terry, Ed Ratleff and George Trapp. *Courtesy of Long Beach State Athletics.*

Hall-of-Famer Lute Olson. McDonald help lead the 49ers to a number two national ranking and back-to-back Elite Eight appearances in the NCAA tournament. He joined a talented team that included guard Ed Ratleff, who was one of the members of the U.S. Olympic team, which became famous for refusing silver medals when the Soviets won a controversial Olympic basketball final in 1972. Ratleff would be inducted into the College Basketball Hall of Fame in 2015, and McDonald would go on to become an NBA legend in Boston. But that would come later.

McDonald, raised alongside his three sisters by a single mother in South Central Los Angeles, always liked the idea of playing for an underdog team. Tarkanian promised him that the unheralded Long Beach State could compete with schools like UCLA, which was in the midst of its march to ten NCAA titles in twelve years. McDonald actually liked the fact that Long Beach played its games in the tiny, hot, 2,400-seat Gold Mine gym.

And hot it was. Fans crammed inside the building, constructed in 1958, and screamed their heads off. When that wasn't loud enough, they banged wood blocks together. As the fan count and decibel level rose, the walls would literally sweat. The moisture would run down the sides of the beige building walls just inches away from the pullout wooden bleachers. "It was hotter than hot, louder than loud," remembers former student and later college administrator Gary Little. "It was fun, but you'd come out of there needing a shower." Big games were held in the Long Beach Arena.

Fans were loud and so fierce at times that they'd make a Duke fan blush. For the NCAA tournament, the students had prepared a cheer for UCLA's Bill Walton, the red-haired, seven-foot star center: "Walton, Walton don't be blue, Frankenstein was ugly, too!" The 49ers got upset early in the tournament that year, and Walton never heard that particular cheer from Long Beach State fans. In 1973, the 49ers beat an Al McGuire–led Marquette team 76–66 in front of almost twelve thousand screaming fans. Two years before, Long Beach State had come within three points of beating UCLA in the NCAA West Regional final at the apex of the John Wooden era.

The Gold Mine reminded McDonald of his Jefferson High School gym. A high scorer there, he would become a defensive standout for the 49ers after holding a top University of the Pacific player to six points after that player had scored thirty-three on the 49ers earlier in the season. The Gold Mine game was sold out, and the team put the overflow crowd into another room and ran a video feed.

McDonald was the first in his family to go to college. "I thought you went to college to play sports," he recalled. "My friends who went to college…they never talked about college, they talked about playing basketball." Indeed, one of McDonald's history professors, David Bernstein, said McDonald once told him he was there to play basketball and would not be attending class.

Perhaps not surprisingly, McDonald the student needed prodding at times. When he slacked off once, blowing off practice and school for a week, Tarkanian took him aside and told him to shape up—one more slip up and he was out. McDonald responded that he'd transfer to USC. Go ahead, said Tarkanian. "When he told me that, I knew he was serious," McDonald said. Tarkanian was not known for insisting students take their studies as seriously as basketball. "Behind closed doors, he was different."

Tarkanian was well known for taking chances on players and drawing lots of attention from the NCAA. President Stephen Horn said he subsequently fired Tarkanian, who was on his way to the University of Nevada–Las Vegas anyway. The coach left in his wake a tide of NCAA sanctions for recruiting violations and other improprieties.

McDonald was himself accused of letting someone take his SAT test in Los Angeles. He was eventually cleared and allowed to play, but the team was smacked with penalties for numerous violations, including the use of ineligible players, improper gifts and inappropriate assistance, among them car payments and airline tickets. The recently successful football team was slapped with multiple sanctions, too.

Scholarships were slashed and post-season play banned for three years. Tarkanian's son Danny and other supporters maintain the NCAA came down with over-the-top penalties to get back at Tarkanian for publicly calling it out for targeting smaller schools and for daring to suit up a higher-than-average number of black players for the time.

In any case, the high-flying days were history. The team went 24-2 during McDonald's last season, when he played for coach Lute Olson. Some believe this was the legendary coach's finest season (he would move on to Iowa and then Arizona, where he would stay for twenty-five years). But the 49ers were put on probation at midseason and barred from the NCAA tournament. Olson stayed only one season.

The 49ers graduated four basketball players who were picked in the NBA's first round. McDonald was selected by the Celtics. He mostly sat on the bench, and that's where he was on June 4, 1976, when his team was locked in a triple-overtime struggle against the Phoenix Suns. It was almost midnight in the Boston Garden and the teams were tied, 118–118. The series was tied at two games apiece. Starter Paul Silas had fouled out, the

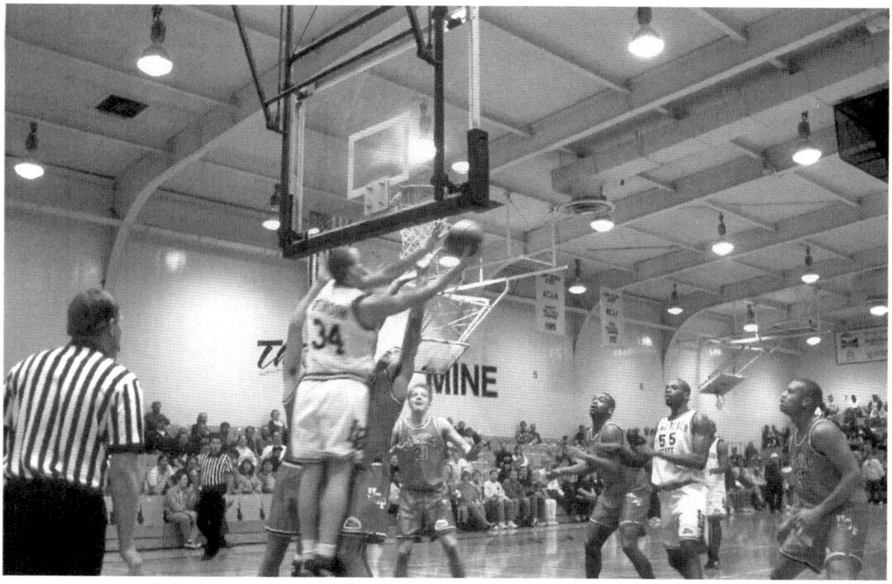

The Gold Mine gym. Especially during the Jerry Tarkanian era, the place was "louder than loud, hotter than hot," said former student and Long Beach State administrator Gary Little. *Courtesy of CSULB.*

fourth Celtics player to do so, and Coach Tommy Heinsohn had a choice. He could go with tough, experienced Steve Kuberski, a strong rebounder, or the less experienced McDonald. With both teams exhausted, he turned to the speedy McDonald.

McDonald thought the coach would choose Kuberski. Then he heard him say "Mac" and he jumped up. "Rarely Used" McDonald came off the bench to score six of the next ten points. He took a pass from Jo Jo White and scored on a quick layup. Then McDonald took a pass from John Havlicek and scored a baseline jump shot, extending the Celtics' lead to four points. McDonald leapt and grabbed a rebound, got fouled and made both free throws, pushing the Celtics ahead by six. The Suns fought back, but the Celtics prevailed, winning 128–126. Delerious fans rushed the court. A victory two nights later gave the team its thirteenth NBA title.

McDonald felt he was doing his job—coming off the bench to help the team. It wasn't until he returned to his apartment in the wee hours of the morning and saw the congratulatory signs his neighbors posted that it all sunk in. "After all the excitement, your body is tingling and you finally relax, then it's like DANG, what did I just do?"

The kid from South Central from the unheralded California program was a Boston hero. That heady feeling didn't last too long; he quickly learned about the business side of pro basketball. He went back home to California, got married and then Heinsohn cut him. "I never knew what it was...I always worked hard. I'd see him when I go back to Boston, he laughs and jokes and talks," said McDonald. "It's been so long, I really don't care."

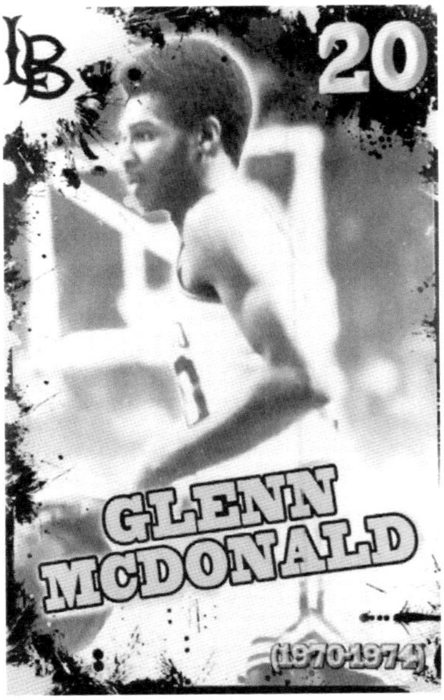

Glenn McDonald was a defensive specialist who became a star for his performance in one playoff game for the Boston Celtics. He initially believed he had come to Long Beach State to play basketball but later returned to get a degree in sociology. *Courtesy of Glenn McDonald.*

He tried to get on with other NBA teams, but it didn't work out. Newly married and eager for job security, he went overseas and enjoyed a good career in Sweden and the Philippines, leading teams to championship seasons. He returned to Long Beach State in 1984 and got his bachelor's, switching to sociology when he realized he didn't have to be a physical education major to coach sports ("I got tired of taking classes in wrestling"). He coached women's basketball for four years, leading the team to a 54-58 record and one NCAA tournament appearance. He later worked as an assistant for the Los Angeles Sparks of the Women's National Basketball Association.

He settled in as director of intramurals at Long Beach State. His son, Michael, played basketball at Stanford. His daughter, Alexis, played at the University of Washington.

Today, McDonald has no regrets. "I would do this all over again. The people at Long Beach treated me so well...When I came back ten years later, people told me, Glenn, you gotta get your degree. A lot of people would just have let it go."

Fans still remember the underdog who came off the bench in the eleventh hour. To this day, McDonald can pick up the phone and get free tickets to see the Celtics, for himself when he's in town or for his son, who works in Boston. "I was not a superstar, but they sure remember that one game!"

9

Play Days

"They Were Forceful Women"

When Dorothy Deatherage showed up for her first physical education instructor's meeting in the fall of 1955, she was dressed in a formal hat and white gloves. But sitting in her car outside the Little Theater on campus, waiting to go in, she watched a parade of female physical education (PE) instructors and professors. They were dressed casually, in comfortable, sporty clothes. So "off came the hat, and off came the gloves," and she went in to join them.

When it came to women's sports, Long Beach State was always ready to play—and not just on the field. The young college had strong administrators willing to fight for money for its PE curriculum and, eventually, gym time for a nascent women's intercollegiate program.

Women's sports would grow from a shoestring operation of play days and dance classes on a dirt lot to a thriving physical education program and, eventually, to a top intercollegiate sports program that has, at times, overshadowed the men's.

The women who brought it there used their own combinations of professionalism, likability, tenacity and bravado. They started the push for equality decades before the 1972 enactment of Title IX, which required that schools provide equal treatment for men and women.

But first, the women's program had to get going in the white glove era of the 1950s. A history of the college's first ten years showed that, by 1959, the college could boast "a full program of intercollegiate athletics" of eleven sports, none of which accommodated women.

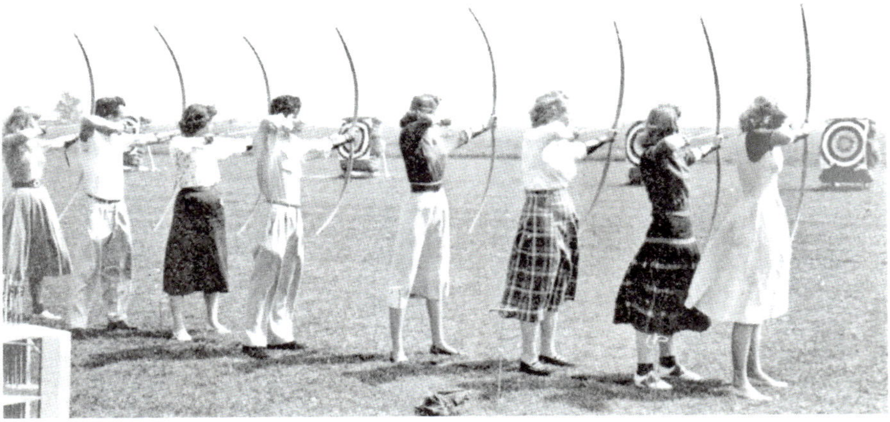

Physical education classes for men and women had to make do with scarce resources in the early days. *Courtesy of CSULB.*

The soft-spoken, golf-loving Deatherage, who was hired away from her job teaching PE at nearby Wilson High School, managed to join a strong staff of doctorate-holding female administrators. The Long Beach native long expected to become a PE teacher and went to school at Stanford and USC, where she eventually earned her own doctorate.

Deatherage originally pooh-poohed the idea of joining her local college after she learned the fledgling women's PE department stored its equipment in a bathtub. But C. Patricia Reid, then a PE instructor in charge of recruiting new teachers, lured her to the campus. A meeting with President P. Victor Peterson and a golf game with the head of the college's Physical Education Department helped ease Deatherage's mind about coming to Long Beach State.

Reid later became chair of the Women's Physical Education Department. The women had to overcome some apathy on campus and, like everyone else, a notable lack of facilities. Women practiced dancing and gymnastics on a dirt lot. They used the Plunge at the Long Beach Pike amusement park for swimming.

A petite woman, Reid was friendly, personable and easy to get along with. And she was never afraid to stand up for women's physical education and, eventually, women's athletics.

When the first gym opened in the mid-1950s, the men took it over, and the women pretty much played sports outside. But when the "big, beautiful men's gym," often called the West Gym, was finished in 1958, the women

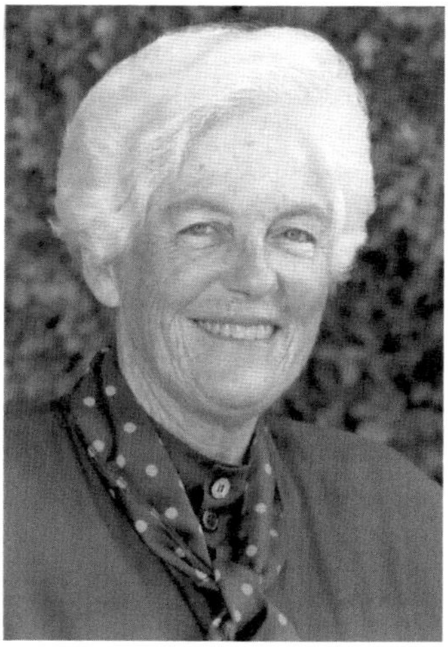

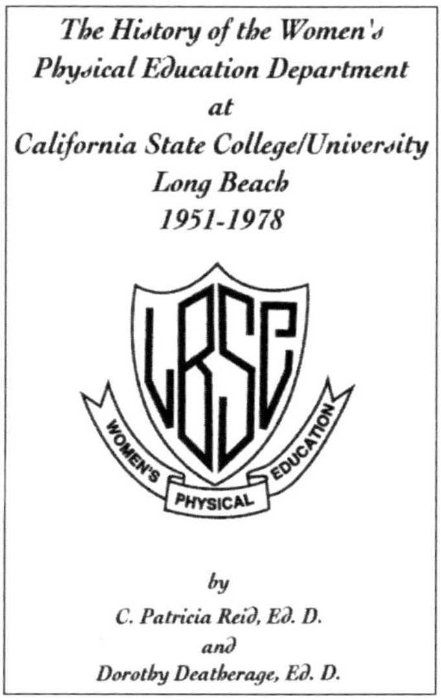

The History of the Women's Physical Education Department at California State College/University Long Beach 1951-1978

by
C. Patricia Reid, Ed. D.
and
Dorothy Deatherage, Ed. D.

Top: Dorothy Deatherage took over women's intercollegiate athletics in 1964, when it had a $400 budget. She just kept asking for more money. *Courtesy of the University Archives.*

Bottom: Dorothy Deatherage and Pat Reid penned a history and guide to women's physical education and athletics that was among the first of its kind. *Courtesy of Dorothy Deatherage.*

got control of the old East Gym. The men still wanted to use that gym, for basketball and other sports that were spilling over. They had to ask Reid, who told them sorry, the gym was scheduled for ladies' sports. That response "was not too well received."

"The program wasn't very big and wasn't very good," Reid recalled later, "but we had a program and we were going to develop it." When women's intercollegiate sports were starting out in the 1960s, Reid "spent a good amount of time convincing the president that it would boost the whole program to hire women and not just another male coach," Deatherage recalled.

The women's intercollegiate program organized "play days" of organized games with other schools. Those later grew into an extramural program that traveled to compete—once, a group of women went to Los Angeles State College to play a team that included Billie Jean King (née Moffitt).

Deatherage took over women's intercollegiate athletics in 1964 with a budget of $400. "There was no Title IX , no nothing," Deatherage recalled. "We would each year make our appeal to the ASI board of control. We spent a lot of time developing budget proposals to show how the money was spent. Nobody cared in those days. They weren't in a position where they could ever care about women's sports. But every year we made our pitch, and our money would grow."

The Associated Students board of control might have gotten "sick of hearing from" Deatherage, but it slowly started handing out money for tennis competitions in Ojai, for instance. The program grew and slowly added sports and, more quickly, victories.

The women's volleyball team started winning in the 1960s and '70s under coach Dixie Grimmett, who won two national championships in the early 1970s under the old Association for Intercollegiate Athletics for Women. The basketball team started building a following under Fran Schaafsma, who compiled at 208-73 record. Schaafsma also, for a time, coached volleyball and basketball at the same time, both to lopsided winning records.

So pure was the women's love of sport, they initially rejected the idea of recruiting talent, said former athletic director Perry Moore. The women saw the men's program's football and basketball reprobation from the NCAA and wanted none of it. But women's sports would embrace recruiting soon enough.

In 1979, assistant Joan Bonvicini was elevated to head basketball coach, and soon the women's games moved over to the bigger West Gym, which was dubbed the Gold Mine. Bonvicini, one of five kids from a Connecticut working-class family, took over the Long Beach program at age twenty-five, becoming one of the youngest head coaches in the country.

"I really loved basketball," Bonvicini told the *Los Angeles Times* in 1989. "I went to 12 years of parochial school because the public schools were so rough, and also because only the Catholic schools had basketball teams. I'll never forget playing in those pleated skirts. I'll tell you, you have to be pretty good to play basketball in a skirt."

Bonvicini's team played an up-tempo game that was ahead of its time and fun to watch. She was also a persistent and fearless recruiter who landed at least one All-American every year, steering them away from bigger and better-funded UCLA, USC and other western schools.

One of those recruits was LaTaunya Pollard, who verbally committed to Long Beach State before changing her mind, saying she would go to UNLV instead. Bonvicini went in to see athletic director Perry Moore.

She told Moore she needed money right away for the redeye flight to East Chicago, Indiana, Pollard's hometown. "I told him I needed to fly back to see this girl and talk to her high school coach," Bonvicini said. "He said you are not going to get her. I told him I promise you I will get this girl, and I promise you this place will be sold out."

Moore agreed. Bonvicini boarded the flight, and Pollard changed her mind and came to Long Beach. She won the Wade Trophy for the best college player in the nation in 1983 and provided part of the nucleus that launched a streak of success—ten Big West championships and twelve NCAA tournament appearances. Long Beach State was one of the first women's programs to be televised on the new Prime Ticket cable schedule in the 1980s.

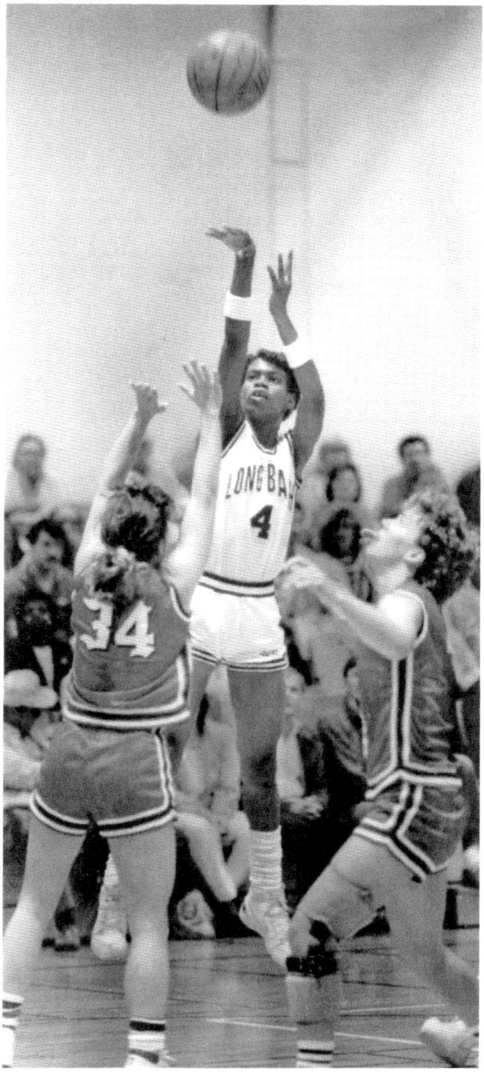

Penny Toler was a star guard for Long Beach State who went on to play for the Los Angeles Sparks. As the general manager, she helped guide the team to two WNBA championships. *Courtesy of Long Beach State Athletics.*

Bonvicini became known for her brash style. When teams complained she was running up the score, she told them to find better players. When the Russian women's team came to town for a series of exhibition games in the 1980s, the 49ers beat them on a late basket. This happened after the Russians beat Los Angeles area teams by thirty or more points. The Russian coach groused about the game immediately after, saying if the teams played the next day, the Russian team would win easily. That's when Bonvicini piped up, "The problem is we're not playing them tomorrow. That's why we beat them today."

The Long Beach State women's team never won a national championship but did make it to the Final Four twice under teams led by Penny Toler, a transfer from San Diego State who would go on to become executive vice-president and general manager of the Los Angeles Sparks. She said the intensely competitive Bonvicini encouraged players to be creative on the court and was just fun to play for. "One thing I would say about Joan, she was funny and she had a great personality," Toler said. "The thing that was always her secret weapon is that she was warm. She was one hell of recruiter and had the gift of gab.

"Here was this white lady going into the inner city to recruit the best basketball players, players who could go to USC and UCLA. They had the Sports Arena and the Wooden Center, and we had this tiny gym, and she had the top five kids coming out of high school. Think about what I'm saying. NC State and Louisiana Tech—here comes Joan, and she can take that player right out of your mouth. She was warm and likable, and that's how she got the recruits."

Bonvicini was making Long Beach State into a national power, and her name was mentioned along with that of Pat Head Summitt, the legendary Tennessee coach. Other schools were making offers. Bonvicini eventually left Long Beach to coach at the more prestigious University of Arizona in 1989. There she endured the triumph and heartbreak of the big-time Pac-10 program, coaching the team to its best record ever—and also getting fired after watching it struggle for three seasons.

In 2009, she became head coach at Seattle University. She said Long Beach State was always her favorite place to coach, saying she "loved it, loved living there, loved everything about" her job there. "Long Beach was way ahead of the curve in a lot of ways with women's athletics."

Glenn McDonald, a Long Beach State basketball star when the men's team was the talk of the campus in the early 1970s, found that when he returned to coach the women's team in the 1980s, things had changed. They weren't talking about the men's team so much. "It was kind of embarrassing," he said. "When you talked about Long Beach State, people would say, 'Oh yeah, the women's basketball team was so good and the women's volleyball team would just fill the stands!'"

Gary Little, a former athlete and longtime booster who often sat in the hot, cramped Gold Mine bleachers to watch the women's games, agreed. "Dorothy [Deatherage] and Fran [Schaafsma] and others were responsible for building a really strong women's program before Title IX, and they were forceful women," Little said.

They were also organized women. In the 1960s, Deatherage helped put together summer sports camps for young athletes, making Long Beach State one of the first colleges to do so. The goal was to train young coaches who would join the public schools.

The camps also served as a prime recruiting ground for young athletes. One of the best known of those was a volleyball player named Misty May.

10

That Championship Season

"No Instant of Negative Thought"

The girls sitting in the bleachers at Long Beach State summer volleyball camp gathered in little groups listening, making friends and setting plans for sleepovers. There was one girl who wasn't chatting much. She was listening attentively. Thirteen-year-old Misty May sat up front by herself as Coach Brian Gimmillaro explained proper setting and spiking. "It was pretty impressive," Gimmillaro recalled. Other girls loved volleyball, too; many of them sat up and paid attention, "but not like that."

The product of two beach volleyball–playing parents, May was a regular at Muscle Beach even as a baby. Volleyball legend Karch Kiraly babysat young Misty when her parents were playing doubles matches.

May grew up to be a versatile, highly competitive athlete, and it wasn't long before she started dreaming of being the female Karch Kiraly and pursuing her own pro volleyball career. The Newport Harbor sophomore was about to be one of the top recruits in the nation. She could go to any school she wanted, and she chose Long Beach State. She remembered the summer camps. She liked the campus and the coaches she got to know at camp, including Gimmillaro and setters' coach Debbie Green, who was considered one of the best in the country.

So before her junior year, May picked up the phone and told Gimmillaro she was committing to Long Beach. Gimmillaro was surprised, to put it mildly, as May wrote in her autobiography:

You would've thought the first words out of his mouth would have been, "Yippee! I've just landed the number one recruit in the country!" Instead he said, "Who's playing a prank on me?"

She wasn't. May signed on at Long Beach for a lot of reasons non-athletes do: her parents lived twenty minutes away in Costa Mesa, so she could eat home-cooked meals and get her wash done, and her volleyball-loving parents could watch her play. The five-foot, nine-inch May wanted to become a setter, and Coach Green, who had considered going back to lead the "normal life" of a mom, decided to stick around, partly because she felt May "was going to be so good, and I wanted to work with her."

In volleyball, the setter is like the quarterback of the team, placing the ball in just the right spot for her teammates to hammer it over the net. May took over the job as a freshman, which was also unusual. She grew into the role and became a maestro at the position. Highly athletic with a keen court sense, she could change her set to suit the hitters and alter her body position and ball placement to confuse the other team.

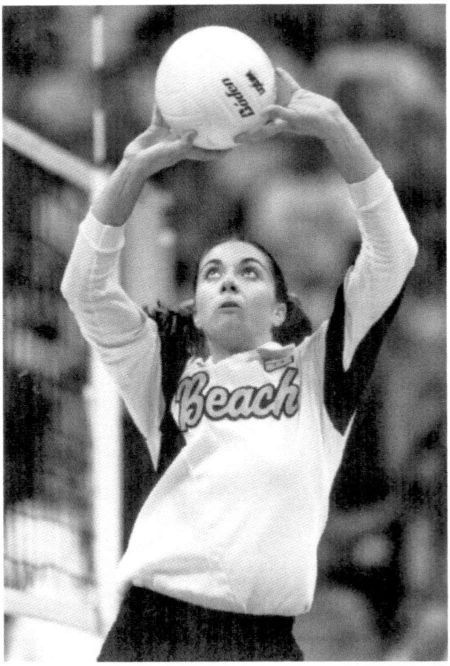

Misty May came to Long Beach State because of the volleyball camps. She came back to join the team because she wanted to play for the coaches she met when she was thirteen. *Courtesy of Long Beach State Athletics.*

"She was by far the best player," said Melissa Ohta, a defensive specialist on the team. "She and Debbie were working every day on something. She kept getting better and better, and you didn't think she could get much better." As setter, May learned to lecture, cajole or amuse her teammates in such a way that she became "better than anyone else at making her fellow players better," according to Gimmillaro.

Women's volleyball had already become popular on the Long Beach campus. Two previous NCAA national championships, in 1989 and 1993 behind Tara Cross-Battle and Danielle Scott, helped with that. But May and the 1998 team gave Long Beach State something it hadn't seen before or since—a perfect 36-0 season, along with an NCAA national championship. That historic season grew out of crushing disappointment in the locker room of the Spokane Arena in Washington State the year before. A relentless Stanford team had just beaten Long Beach State in the semifinals in December 1997.

"Kerri Walsh of Stanford killed herself to beat Long Beach," Gimmillaro said of the player who would become May's future beach volleyball partner. The Long Beach team that spent the 1997 season atop the rankings was nevertheless seeded number two, prompting the match against top-seeded Stanford as well as Brian Gimmillaro's ire.

In the silent locker room after the loss, Gimmillaro asked the women what they wanted next year. May said a national championship. Teammate Jessica Alvarado added that she wanted a perfect season.

After 1997, "we had the team and the intense desire and the feeling of being wronged," Gimmillaro said, "to win in 1998."

And that meant the coach's practices, always grueling, became even more so. Everything had to be perfect—they had to jump higher and get to the ball quicker. It was exhausting. Some players threw up just thinking about it. But after Gimmillaro's awful practices, the games seemed easy. And they were a lot of fun for fans. The 49ers crushed opponents and filled the Pyramid with patrons who got free bagels or In-N-Out burgers if the team won in less than sixty minutes. Young girls and middle-aged men showed up at the games in May's signature pigtails.

In December, the 49ers marched through the NCAA tournament, crushing their first-round opponent in forty-five minutes. They knocked off the University of Florida Gators in the semifinal to win their thirty-fifth match of the season. Next up was Penn State for the final. The Nittany Lions were also 35-0. The records were the same, but the big-time sports pedigrees of the two schools were not. Penn State had a football team and an athletic budget that was eight times that of the 49ers. And it was closer to Madison, the tournament site. While Penn State was a not-insignificant eleven-hour car trip from Madison, Long Beach was a thirty-one-hour car trip away. Consequently, the Long Beach cheering section was small. The Long Beach Athletic Department, unable to fly out the school band, hired the Wisconsin Badger band to play Long Beach State's fight songs.

In the final, the 49ers won the first two games easily, but the Lions came back to win the next two and took an 8–4 lead in the final game. Instead of falling apart as the team had done against Stanford the previous year, the 49ers climbed back. "We were better prepared, and we executed,"

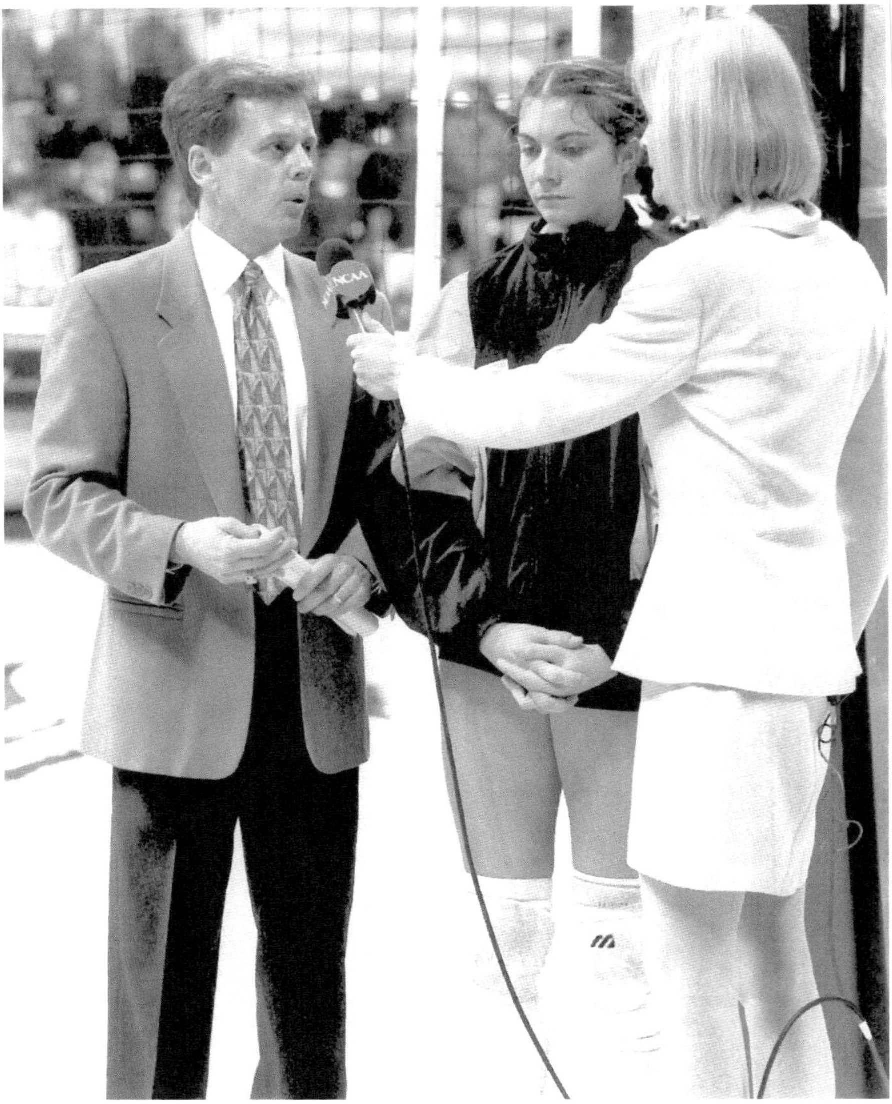

Volleyball coach Brian Gimmallaro and star setter Misty May are interviewed during the NCAA tournament in 1998. *Courtesy of Long Beach State Athletics.*

Gimmillaro said. "We were not gonna' come that far and not win. There was no doubt in my mind we were going to win. I had no fear of not winning, no instant of negative thought."

May agreed the team had reached that nearly perfect celestial plane of competitive confidence. "We were like the little train that kept plugging away," she said. "It would have been nice to win in three. We had our chances. We never doubted, and we just kept doing. There was no panic, there was a calm, like everything was going to be fine."

Gimmillaro said he didn't know the team was behind until a reporter pointed it out after the match. At game point, May served, the ball came back over the net, and May set it up for Veronica Walls, who sent a hard shot over the net for the final point.

The team that had been so balanced, so businesslike, jumped up and down like cheerleaders while the hired Wisconsin band played. "We were just relieved," said teammate Melissa Ohta, who went on to coach at the University of Arizona. "Everything you did was completely worth it, and being so disappointed the year before made it twice as good. It was the best feeling…that it was all worth it. You don't get to say that often in life."

Gimmillaro leapt into a player's arms and raised his fist. "Volleyball is different," Gimmillaro said later. "In football you're ahead, you know you're going to win…also basketball relies on the clock. If you're ahead when it runs out, you win. In volleyball, you have to score the last point. There is no time to prepare for that feeling of being a champion. You cannot get into the

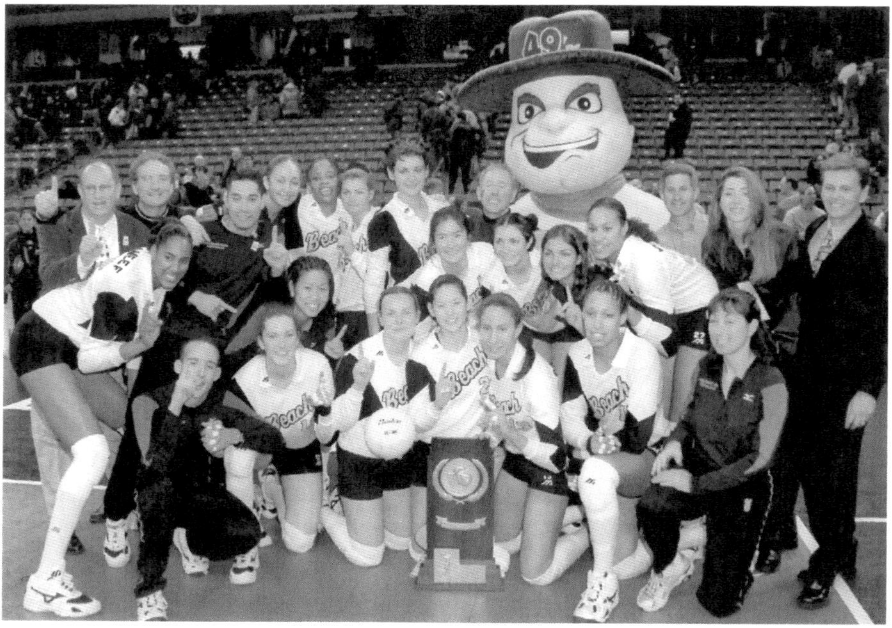

The team poses with its NCAA champion trophy after winning in 1998. President Robert Maxson is in the back, just left of Prospector Pete. Misty May is in front of Maxson, and setter's coach Debbie Green is in front at right. *Courtesy of CSULB.*

feeling of being a champion until it happens. That fact defines how intense that celebration is."

The *Press-Telegram* headline said, "Perfection." The 49ers won 15–3, 15–10, 13–15, 14–16, 15–12 in front of 13,194 people, the largest crowd to watch an NCAA volleyball match. It was a record that stood for five years. May was named co-MVP of the tournament, setting an NCAA record with twenty service aces. She was also named the American Volleyball Coaches Association Player of the Year for the second year in a row, the first consecutive AVCA winner since Long Beach State's Tara Cross in 1989–90.

The winner's parade of events was next. The team threw out the first pitch at a Dodger's game and was featured at halftime at the Lakers game. They met President Bill Clinton by Air Force One on the LAX tarmac. May became a superstar in beach volleyball, winning three gold medals with former tournament foe Kerri Walsh.

May has said she misses indoor volleyball. "There was nothing like the women I shared college experience with," said May, who lives with her husband, Matt Treanor, in Long Beach. "It showed as a team we set a goal, and everyone made that decision to follow through. Every time I see it I get goose bumps…it meant the world to us and still does."

11

Robert Maxson

"He Woke Us Up"

The Long Beach State campus in the early '90s was a little down in the dumps. The football team had packed up for good in 1991, professors were leaving with golden parachute contracts and budget cuts were leading to higher fees and trimmed class schedules. After years of explosive growth, Long Beach State was losing enrollment and hanging near the bottom of the *U.S. News and World Report* rankings.

President Curtis McCray left in 1994 after four and a half years, disappointing many and adding to the *ennui*. When Robert Maxson interviewed for the president's job, he saw a campus that "needed a big hug."

"I just sensed I came to a good place; nothing needed to be fixed, there was good faculty and staff," Maxson said. "It just needed a big hug and to be told 'you're good.'"

After years of steadily, often dramatically, rising enrollment, the number of students fell more than 12 percent from 1992 to 1994, to 26,277—largely because of admission restrictions due to budget cuts. The six-year graduation rate was around 30 percent (half what it would be by the mid-2010s), and courses, sports and teaching positions were slashed while fees were rising.

Meanwhile, 284 miles away at the University of Nevada–Las Vegas, President Robert Maxson was pretty battle-scarred himself after years spent tussling with UNLV legendary basketball coach Jerry Tarkanian. The enormously successful coach was constantly dodging very determined NCAA investigators and had been hard put to explain why three of his players were photographed sharing a hot tub with a convicted point shaver.

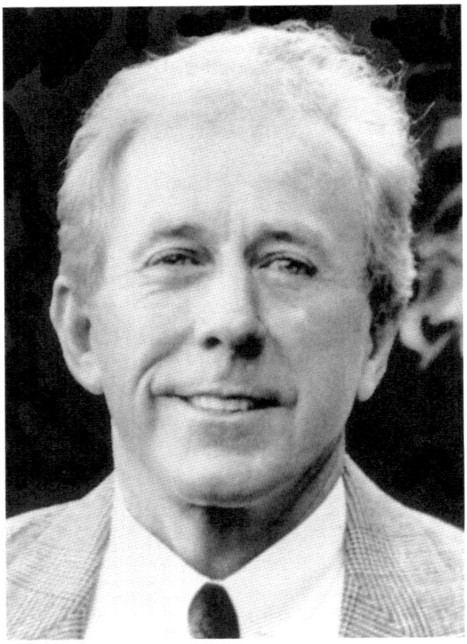

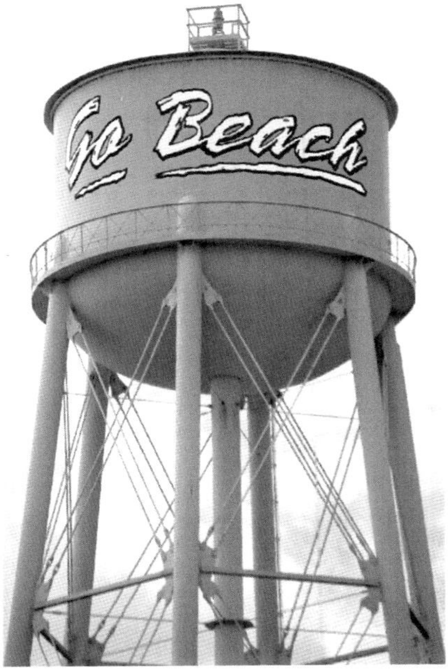

Left: Robert Maxson in 1994. He said the campus at the time seemed to need "a big hug." *Courtesy of CSULB.*

Right: Maxson didn't come up with the "Beach" nickname, but he popularized it—punctuating every speech and slapping the logo on any available bare surface. The Veterans Administration water tower was no exception. *Courtesy of CSULB.*

Maxson eventually drove Tarkanian out, which didn't help Maxson's standing with powerful UNLV sports boosters. He left for a fresh start at Long Beach State.

By all accounts, he got it. When he arrived in 1994, the campus was quickly charmed by the fifty-nine-year-old's buttery Arkansas accent, his tendency to hug, his frequent strolls around campus and boundless optimism. "He came to campus and walked around and said, 'These people are just depressed,'" recalled Doug Robinson, the former vice-president of student services. "He knew that his job was to promote the campus."

First, he found a rallying cry. He took the "Beach" nickname and ran with it. He started punctuating his speeches with "Go Beach!" He greeted students on campus that way. And they started answering "Go Beach!" back.

Like a cheerleading tagger, Maxson slapped "The Beach" on any free space he could find—even the water tower at the Veterans Administration hospital, which looms over the campus. "First they said no, they were afraid rival teams would climb up there and mark on it," Maxson said.

Eventually, student body president Robert Garcia asked if the student government could paint "Go Beach" on the bottom of the student union pool. Maxson said fine, if they could find the money. The student, who would eventually become mayor of Long Beach, saw to it that the pool was drained, painted and filled up again. "I'm not sure it made any academic departments better," Maxson said. "But I think student morale benefited. They would go to trustees meetings, and our student body president would give a report—'Thank you for having me and Go Beach!' We got known for that 'round the CSU system."

Long Beach State was also known then as a campus that attracted an older, part-time student body and others who saw the east Long Beach campus as a third- or fourth-choice institution. Maxson attempted to change that by offering high school valedictorians a chance to attend Long Beach State for free—room, board and fees all paid. He started the program at UNLV when he saw Nevada's best and brightest were leaving the Silver State. Maxson convinced a casino magnate to kick in $1 million to get the program started.

At Long Beach State, faculty members were skeptical. "When he first announced it, we were thinking, 'How's he going to get valedictorians to come to CSULB?'" recalls Dee Abrahamse, then an administrator with the College of Liberal Arts. "They're going to go to UCLA and Berkeley."

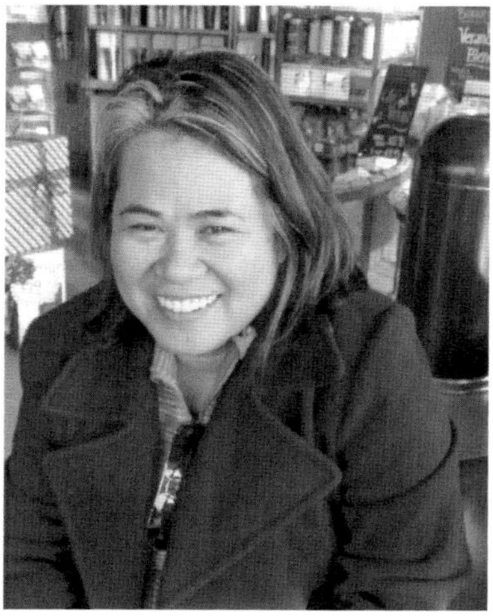

Dianne Asis, a valedictorian from Long Beach Jordan High School, now works with a private investment firm. She had no plans to attend Long Beach State but changed her mind when she got the chance to go there for free with the first president's scholars class. *Author photo.*

Students weren't much more receptive but enough of them came around. Dianne Asis, a valedictorian at Long Beach's Jordan High School in a working-class section of Long Beach, was hoping to attend the University of California, Irvine. Then her counselor mentioned she had a chance to go to Long Beach State for free. "I wasn't even considering it," said Asis, who went into computer engineering and now works for a private investment firm in Los Angeles. "But once I met President Maxson...as soon as you meet him, you're on board with everything he says...He said, 'We're gonna' bring in best and brightest.'...I was one of the best and brightest! These people around me [in the scholar's program] are geniuses. I'm in company with them, and I'm from Jordan High."

Maxson introduced the first president's scholars class of ten students in the student union ballrooms in the fall of 1995. "They got a standing ovation," recalls Valerie Bordeaux, who has run the program since its inception. "Everyone went wild." Maxson also made sure to include the scholars' parents in the ceremony.

"He understood the sports concept where you recruit the family not just the students," Robinson said. "He'd have all those parents up there and drip honey on them just as he dripped honey on the students. He was playing to the university community, and he knew the media would be there."

Maxson, who never cared much about traveling for the job, stuck around and led the cheers for Long Beach State every chance he got. "He walked the walk and talked the talk," Bordeaux said. "He made it a priority, every meeting he led and every organization he spoke to, he was talking about that program." Headlines such as "The Beach Is Back!" showed up in

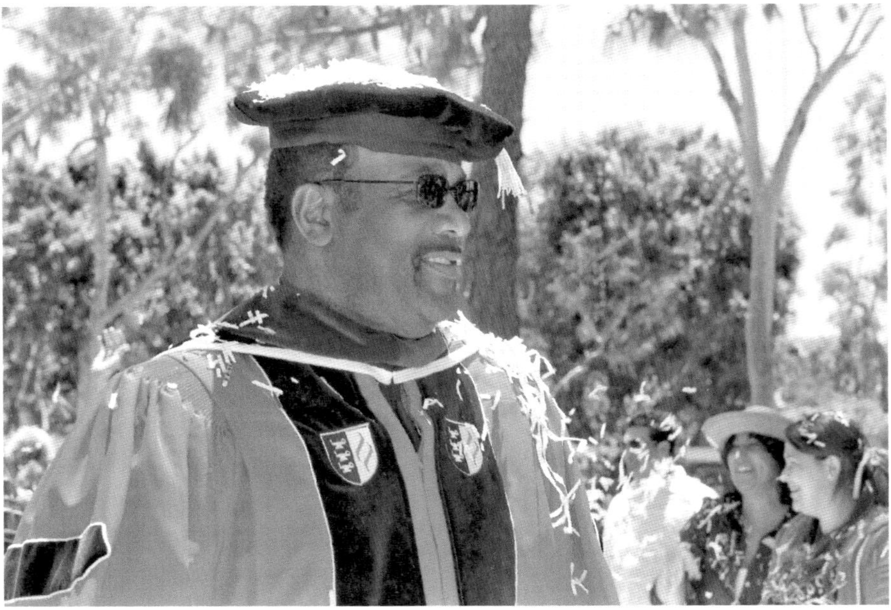

Doug Robinson, the vice-president for student services who worked closely with Maxson, said the president understood that he had to get parents to buy into the president's scholars program. It was not a hard sell. *Courtesy of CSULB.*

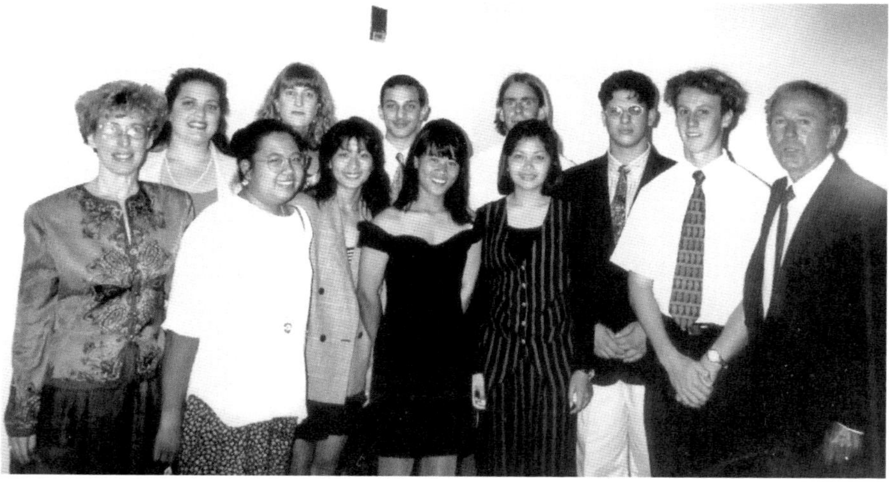

The first president's scholars class. Robert Maxson is at the far right. Dianne Asis is in the front row in the black dress, with her hands behind her back. *Courtesy of the President's Scholars Program.*

publications. One of those was the *U.S. News and World Report*, the college-rating publication that administrators pretend to hate while they fight their way to the top of it. The university bean counters learned they had been incorrectly submitting graduation and other statistics indicating university health and well-being. They learned to submit numbers that highlighted the university's selling points.

Meanwhile, more and more president's scholars were landing on campus, and university officials learned that students who didn't get in on a full scholarship would enroll anyway and "ride the coattails of the president's scholars," Robinson said.

Slowly, the median campus age came down, and more students started seeing the Beach as a destination rather than a school of convenience. Maxson said that when he arrived at Long Beach State, it was "mainly known as a university of part-time students, a university of older students. Both of those are fine; we cherish those returning students. We just wanted our share of best and brightest. If you're always the third or fourth choice, you're never going to be a very good university."

University enrollment beefed up again in the late '90s, and the university started to sneak up in the *U.S. News and World Report* rankings, until Long Beach State's routinely high ranking stopped becoming news.

Relations between faculty and the president's office, which had been rocky and occasionally hostile for decades, smoothed considerably during the Maxson years. When he retired, the president of the Academic Senate made a joke about cloning him.

Maxson "doesn't get near enough credit for changing the culture of the campus," said Scott Charmack, who spent twenty-five years with facilities and physical planning. "We were a sleeping giant, and he woke us up," says Bordeaux. "He gave those hugs and told the stories and he woke us up."

12

The Pyramid

A Cheap Icon

When architect Donald Gibbs was bent over blueprints, planning what would become the university's most iconic structure, he was still recovering from his biggest professional heartache. The roof of the nearby campus recital hall that Gibbs had designed had collapsed on July 2, 1990, dropping 120 tons of concrete onto the seats and flattening two Steinway grand pianos. No one was in the building at the time. If anyone had been, they would have been crushed.

Gibbs, then fifty-six, had hired the structural engineer, whom he said fled after the collapse. The whole episode, he said, "was devastating."

The university sued Gibbs's firm, as well as the contractor and maker of the roof trusses that gave way. While no one was hurt, the collapse forced the displacement of scores of classes. Scheduled concerts were dispersed to local churches. The case was eventually settled out of court.

Jon Regnier, the associate vice-president for physical planning who was involved in the investigation of the collapse, said the builder bore most of the responsibility for the crash. Regnier said a series of errors led to the collapse, including the fact the contractor missed an entire row of nails that were supposed to secure the trusses, which eventually gave way.

Nevertheless, the collapse marked the low point of Gibbs's sixty-year career and, for a time, a blemish for a family steeped in Long Beach architecture. Gibbs's father, Hugh, drew up Long Beach State's first campus master plan in the mid-1950s, when the state still held control over the campus look and budget. Gibbs himself designed the psychology building as well as Long

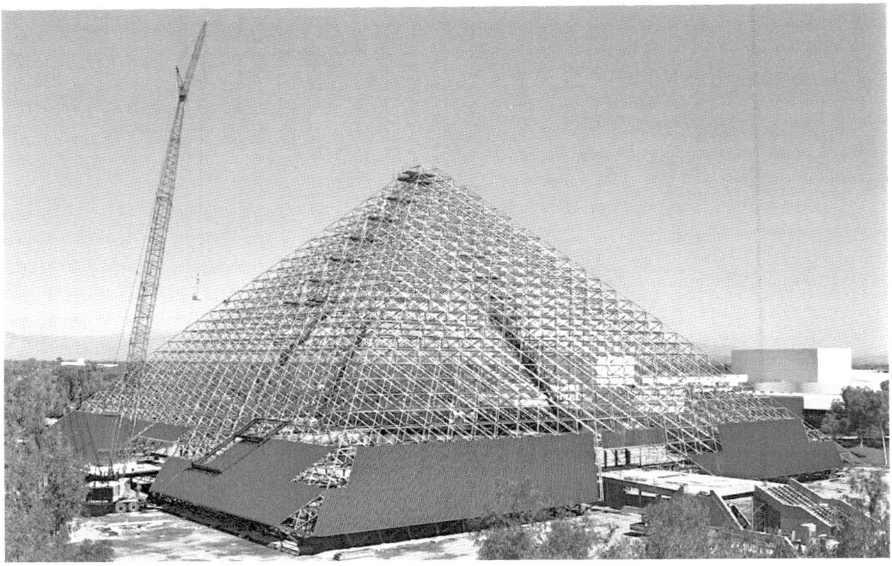

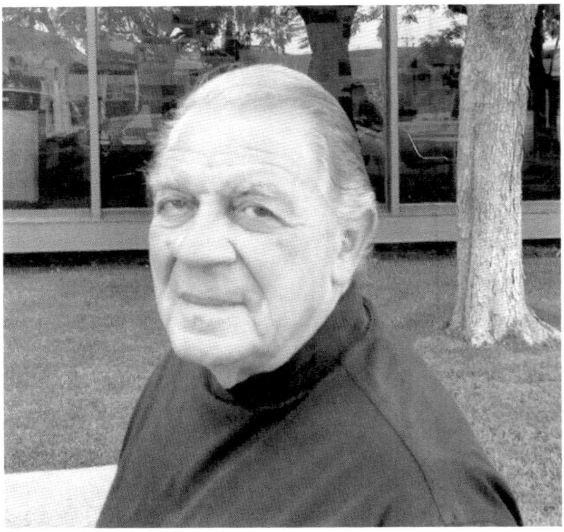

Above: The Pyramid under construction in 1994. Delays pushed the opening date to November 1994, and officials struggled to secure funding. *Courtesy of CSULB.*

Right: Don Gibbs outside his Bixby Knolls architecture firm. He designed the Walter Pyramid, the Richard and Karen Carpenter Performing Arts Center, the psychology building and Long Beach City Hall. *Author photo.*

Beach City Hall and scores of other structures. At the time of the collapse, he was under contract to design a new physical education building and also a performing arts venue at the college that would become the Richard and Karen Carpenter Performing Arts Center.

Gibbs pressed on, turning his sights on Paris, specifically, the Louvre. Gibbs was entranced by the landmark museum and its glass-and-metal pyramid entrance designed by I.M. Pei that stands in stark contrast to the over two-hundred-year-old museum courtyard.

A fan of geometric abstractions, Gibbs felt a pyramid was just the thing to give Long Beach State, then reeling from budget and enrollment cuts, the statement he thought the campus needed. Gibbs took the plan to President Curtis McCray. The president's response was something along the lines of "You want to do *what*, Don?" Still, the 1978 and 1988 master plans called for some kind of arena on the northern end of campus. Officials quickly embraced the idea of a big-splash structure that would bookend with the nine-story McIntosh building on the campus's southern end.

The issue, as it always was and will be in the state system, was cost. The state had only recently—in 1988—started allowing money to flow to "PE projects" as opposed to strictly academic ones. Five physical education projects were approved for the CSU system in 1990. However, voters refused to pass a bond to finance them. That meant the buildings would have to be done cheaply or not at all.

Campus officials, aware that the Athletic Department was tired of the sweaty and cramped Gold Mine gym, were willing to try. School officials visited arenas in Berkeley, Davis, Irvine and San Jose. They considered a domed arena. The Long Beach State athletic director at the time suggested moving to campus the cavernous geodesic dome in Long Beach Harbor that once housed the Hughes Flying Boat, the Spruce Goose. All ideas ended up being far too costly.

Gibbs moved ahead with his Pyramid, an arena that would seat 7,500, although only about 5,000 seats went in, to save money. The seats would be close to the court, and at the request of the campus associate vice-president for physical planning, Jon Regnier, hydraulic lifts would be installed for the seats, eliminating time spent pulling out bleachers, as was the procedure for every Gold Mine contest. Gibbs drew in more room for basketball courts and a nice sixty-foot ceiling that would warm the heart of volleyball recruits who remembered all those trapped balls in high school gym rafters.

As for the color, Gibbs would have loved to have used copper, but again, that cost too much money. Instead, he designed a special corrugated steel shape for the roof, painted with a special blue, galvanized paint designed to last twenty-five years. The deep blue color would blend with the sky, and the frame was so light that it reduced the cost of the footings to support the structure.

Construction snafus surfaced. A contractor over-drilled fasteners to the roof, and another contractor installed the corrugated steel with seams on the bottom, allowing water to leak in. This prompted more litigation and necessitated thousands of dollars in repairs until the problem was eventually fixed.

The Pyramid was a different kind of building from the start. Instead of sitting parallel to the street like other campus buildings, it would rest at a seven-degree angle. That was his architect son Kurt's idea. Basically, he thought it would look cool that way. Kurt said later, "Buildings are better viewed obliquely anyway. There's no reason to align anything to the gods any more…you know, stay loose, enjoy the ride." Several residents living around the planned construction site were not so sure.

When word got out about a new pyramid-shaped gymnasium, neighbors who remembered the music center roof collapse cracked that the college was finally constructing something the architects and builders could handle: no roof. Some did more than crack dark jokes, though. Alarmed at claims the structure would be eighteen stories high, homeowners circulated a five-hundred-signature petition and complained to their councilmember. Some claimed the pyramid design would constitute a satanic outline. Others quoted passages in the Bible that referred forebodingly to a rising blue pyramid. One man complained that people in the structure would be able to see into his bathroom, until officials explained that there would be no outside windows for anyone to look through.

Still others, more accustomed to living across from a gravel parking lot, said they hated the thought of extra traffic, extra noise and rowdy sports fans celebrating so close by. Neighbors prevailed on campus officials to move the structure one hundred feet back from the street—a last-minute change that cost an extra $180,000. It didn't bug the designer, though.

Gibbs, a tireless worker who would go on to embrace wood sculpture, was proud of his "visual adventure" with no windows, no vents, no interruptions to interfere with the clean blue pyramid lines. The effect, he hoped, would "allow one's mind to run free."

But campus officials' minds were preoccupied with the bills for the $22 million visual adventure. They spoke of getting sponsorship from the Union 76 gasoline company and putting a big orange ball on the top. Gibbs said it was hard to tell if they were kidding or not. Later, they tried to get JetBlue to sponsor the arena. It was blue, after all, and right on the Long Beach Airport flight path, so many a JetBlue pilot flies by it. Airline officials weren't interested.

Eventually, Mike Walter, the former dean of the College of Business Administration and a vice-president of Levi Strauss, Inc., stepped up and donated more than $2 million, prompting others to follow suit for a $5 million total. School officials named it the Walter Pyramid in 2005—happily, for Gibbs, ending the talk of exterior accouterments.

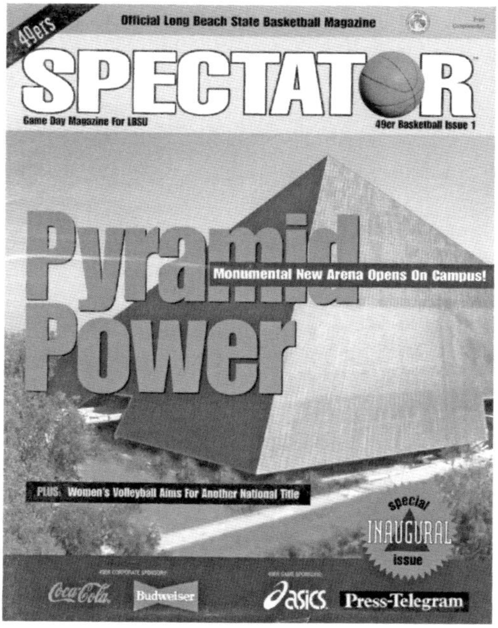

Lots of hoopla greeted the Pyramid opening on November 30, 1994. It became a sought-after venue and a signature building for the campus. *Courtesy of Long Beach State Athletics.*

The Pyramid opened on November 30, 1994, when the men's basketball team hosted Detroit in a nationally televised game. The grand opening was glorious for officials. But when athletic officials hired a spotlight to light the sky around the new Pyramid, the Federal Aviation Administration called to tell them to stop; the light was blinding the pilots trying to land at Long Beach Airport. They shut it down in fifteen minutes.

And for a while, the neighbors' worst fears were realized; fans parked in their neighborhoods, and some of them were loud and rowdy. The neighbors prevailed on the college and the city to enforce parking restrictions. But since then, many homeowners have since learned to live with the sky blue structure in their midst.

"If you talk to people who were freaked out about it being across the street from their homes, they'd say now they kind of like it," said Andy Jones, a neighbor who helped fight the building and now works as associate vice chancellor and deputy general counsel for the Cal State system. "It's kind of a landmark, 'Hey I live by the Pyramid.'"

It can be seen from every point on campus and also the local freeways. Some pilots say that they unofficially use it for visual navigation when they fly into Long Beach Airport. It quickly became a symbol of the university. It appeared on letters, Christmas cards and on the masthead of the campus newspaper. It even became a symbol of the neighborhood; a local realtor put it on his truck.

The Pyramid would become the home of the men's and women's basketball teams and volleyball teams. Players such as Misty May, who remembers "needing a shower" while watching a game in the old Gold Mine, loved playing in the new airy, clean building with its expansive ceiling.

Every time President Robert Maxson saw Gibbs, he told him, "Don, that's not a new building, it's a new beginning." Gibbs watched the Richard and Karen Carpenter Performing Arts Center he designed open for performances with a black-tie gala the same year. The Carpenter Center was modeled after the David H. Koch Theater in the Lincoln Center for the Performing Arts and would become a popular arts venue for the community and the region. It went up a stone's throw from the recital hall that had fallen down four years before.

Still, it was the Pyramid that captured the campus's, and city's, imagination. "Designing something, and seeing it become a symbol for the university," Gibbs said, "is pretty special."

13

Puvungna

The Land Is Sacred

Cindi Alvitre says her grandfather delivered hay to the old Bixby ranch in the 1930s. As father and son rode together in the hay wagon over the land that would become Long Beach State, he would put his finger to his lips.

"Shush," he would say, "this land is sacred."

Alvitre is the director of the Ti'at Society of the Gabrielino Tongva affiliated with the Southern California Indian Community. The lecturer in American Indian studies said the university is part of Puvungna, a large district of sacred land that a millennium ago stretched far inland from the Bolsa Chica area of Huntington Beach.

"We are told that Puvungna is the emergence point of the spiritual philosophy of most Southern California Indian tribes," said Alvitre. "That's the best way to put it. It's where the world emerges and where those creation narratives occur."

Now most of that land is covered with houses, malls and a large university. On campus, all that remains undeveloped is twenty-two acres on its western edge, and memories of a bitter court fight that pitted university lawyers against lawyers representing Native Americans.

The vacant land now consists of mostly overgrown grass, acacia trees and a mix of living and dead peach trees. It is bordered on Bellflower Boulevard by a line of shady trees that give an arbor-like impression to this end of the urban campus. There's an uneven blacktop parking lot on the site and not much else. The grass turns a fertile green in the winter and a withering brown in the summer. In the early '90s, the university

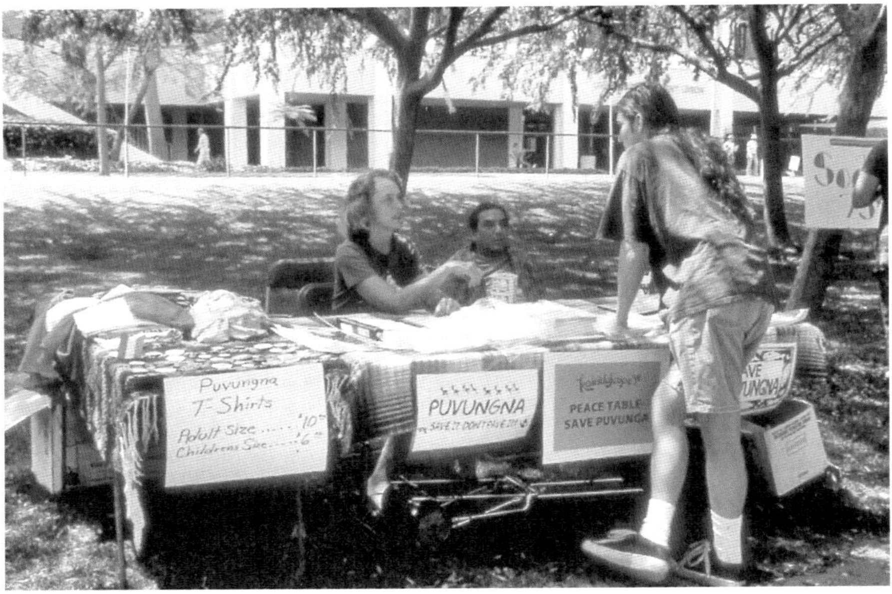

Students sell T-shirts and advocate for saving the twenty-two acres of Puvungna land from development at a table outside the University Student Union during the 1990s. The university's push to build stores and housing on the land became a polarizing issue. *Courtesy of the University Archives.*

saw that patch of land quite differently. University officials made plans to build a complex called the West Village Center, which was to include a commercial/retail area with restaurants and stores. Plans included high-density, below-market-price housing for faculty. Rising on the twenty-two acres, it was to be a public-private partnership, a moneymaker to ease university finances at a time when the institution was under pressure to generate its own funds.

The land appeared to have everything going for it. It was undeveloped and largely unused, except for a thriving organic garden. It was bordered by a heavily trafficked major street and was Park Estates adjacent—next to one of the wealthiest areas of the city. Yet planners failed to account for the land's history of one thousand years ago, a misstep that would pit college administrators against area Native Americans and, in the end, doom the project.

Native Americans won a bitter court battle with the university to protect the land from development. They say Puvungna is sacred to the Gabrielino people, as well as to other neighboring tribes.

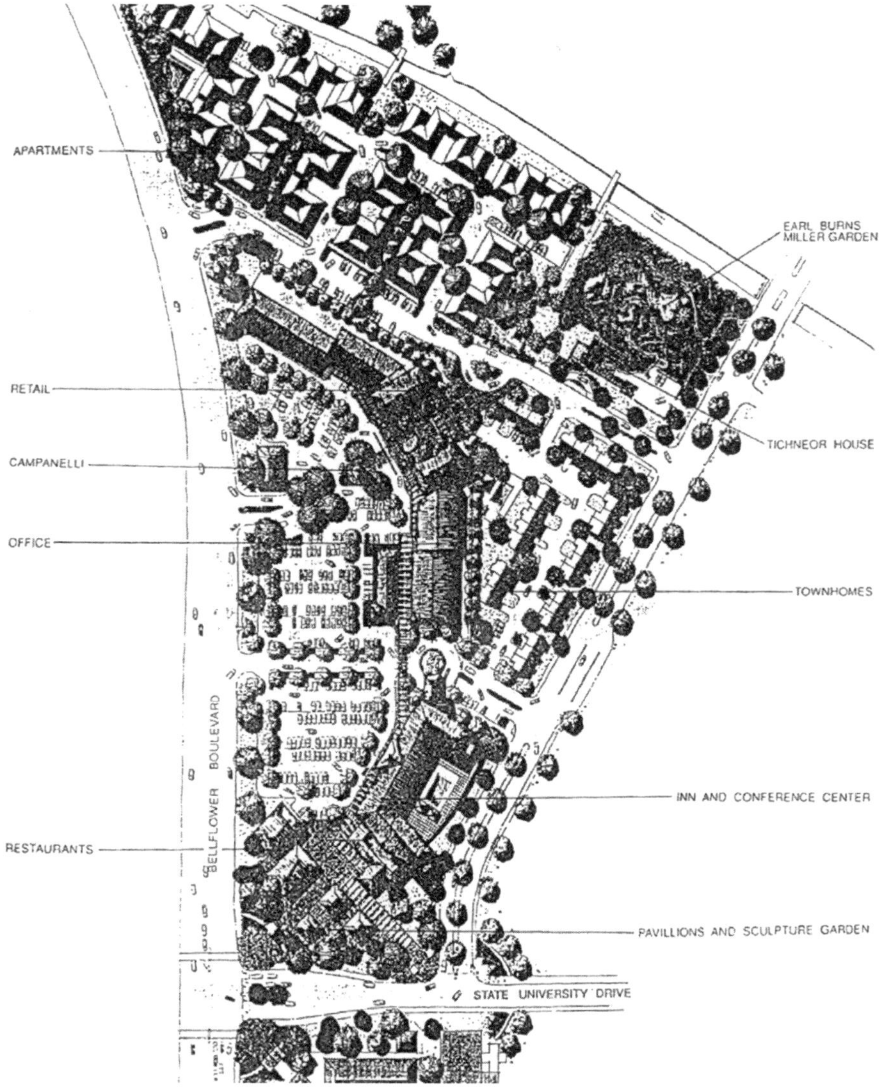

The West Village Center originally called for shopping, restaurants and high-density faculty housing for the twenty-two acres known as Puvungna. The plan ignited a bitter battle between the university and Native Americans in the early 1990s. That land is open today, and the university has no plans to build on it. *Courtesy of the University Archives.*

"Would the Christian communities allow you to urinate on the Shroud of Turin, or build a mini mall in sacred sites in Jerusalem?" Alvitre wrote to interim president Karl Anatol in May 1993. "Well, I say to you…our people will not allow this desecration of our sacred sites, either." Few seemed to embrace the project. Neighbors in Park Estates didn't want the extra traffic and noise the West Village Center would invariably bring.

In the special collections room of the university library, twenty boxes are stuffed with records detailing the struggle over Puvungna, including newspaper stories of protests, courtroom skirmishes and plans proposed and permanently tabled.

On the same patch of land two decades earlier, a maintenance crew discovered a skeleton while installing an irrigation system in the early 1970s.

Anthropology professor Ron Loewe, who was completing a book on the controversy in the spring of 2015 called *Of Sacred Lands and Strip Malls: Indian Wars at Cal State Long Beach 1992 to 1998*, said one source of documentation of Puvungna comes from the writing of a Franciscan missionary by the name of Boscana, who was in charge of the San Juan Capistrano and San Gabriel missions. Boscana wrote that Native Americans told him their prophet appeared in Puvungna, a place described as "11 leagues" north of San Juan Capistrano. That would put Puvungna near Lake Elsinore. But many experts say that's a mistake and that Boscana really meant northwest, meaning the location is actually the site of the Nieto land grant, in east Long Beach and western Orange County.

Jon Regnier, the longtime campus facilities director, said the remains found on the twenty-two acres were properly buried by the International House. He contends that the lack of further known human remains means the university should have built something on the site years ago. "When we dug the Japanese Garden, there was nothing there," he said. "When they dug the channel for the creek, nothing there. When we dug for the International House, there was nothing there." He and others believe the remains found there were probably part of land cleared by the nearby Veterans Administration facility, which was constructed in the 1940s.

The remains of about twenty-three Native American people were found north of campus at the Los Altos shopping center. Workers building houses in the area in 1952 and 1953 found remains dating to the 1200s, and students got involved in the excavation. The area where the shopping center is now was likely a cemetery, Alvitre said.

Most of the human remains have been stored for years in the Liberal Arts 5 building on campus. Alvitre is in charge of the internment and reburying of the remains, which is to take place in 2015 near the International House on Beach Drive, just south of the twenty-two acres.

There is ample evidence of Native Americans who settled, ate and lived on the university land roughly one thousand years ago. According to a May 2013 article in *Pacific Coast Archaeological Society Quarterly*, construction of a parking garage near the Walter Pyramid turned up pottery pieces, stone and bone tools and more than a metric ton of mollusk shells, a popular dining choice of early Native Americans. The site, dated to AD 1200 to AD 1700, contained the best-dated excavated pottery collection from Southern California and "reveals a ceramic industry pre-dating the arrival of Europeans," the article states.

As for the development, the university gave up on it soon after President Robert Maxson took office in 1994. Maxson promised the Native American community he would not build on the land when he was president. He didn't say it would never happen, but he said *he* wouldn't do it. And Maxson hated the idea of a commercial development anyway.

"I don't think you should commercialize a campus," Maxson said in an interview. "A campus is a sacred learning environment. There was a big argument with the Native American community not wanting it developed…there was a move to build stores. There were plans. I was shown plans, and I just said no. It wasn't just a Native American question. As long I was president, I wasn't going to commercialize the campus."

Some say the twenty-two acres of Puvungna land was a sacred site; others say it really wasn't. But there's no question it is now, and that's, in part, because of the outrage that grew from the development that was to have been built there in the early 1990s. Its safe to say there are no such plans on the current president's desk. "As long as I'm president, there will not be any commercial development," President Jane Close Conoley said in 2015. (Alvitre said Conoley is the first president to visit the site of the "ancestors"—the remains about to be reburied on campus.) She notes the current university master plan has nothing going in on that site. "If we do develop it, it would be for university purposes, and I think we have an opportunity and we have a history. We can celebrate the history of that site."

Archeology professor Carl Lipo said the twenty-two acres "has value beyond archeology…That's the only piece of land that isn't a mall or a golf course or a managed park where they plant trees and grass," Lipo said. "It's the last piece of land that reflects the prairie landscape. It's the only place left that has anything to do with the [Native American] past."

So the university land that was once a lightly settled outpost of rural Long Beach now is home to one of the city's last pieces of untouched real estate. And it will likely stay that way, at least for a while.

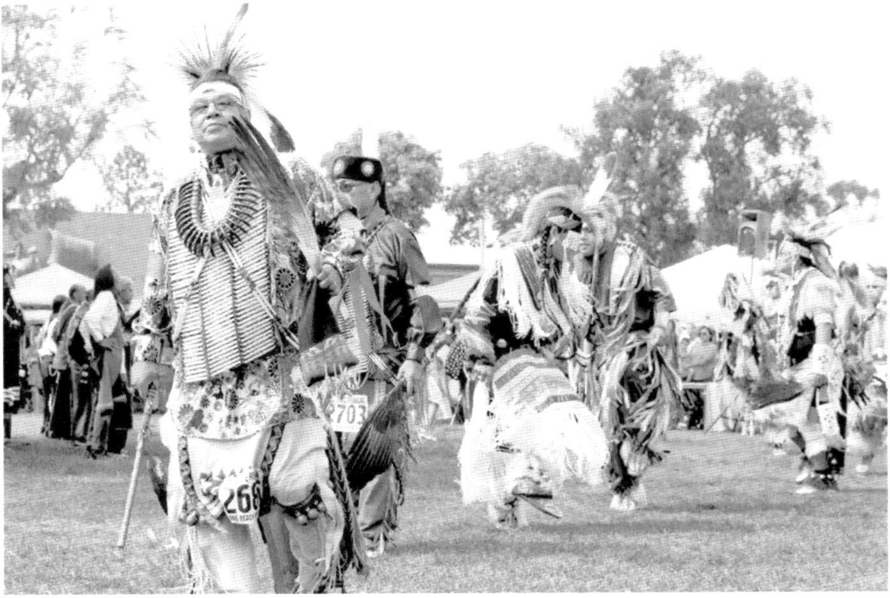

Native Americans dance during the Grand Entry at the Forty-fifth Annual Long Beach Pow Wow on March 15, 2015. The annual celebration attracts thousands to the campus every spring. *Courtesy of Michael Ares and the* Daily 49er.

Alvitre contends that the Native American history of the land influences the university today. She said there are Native American influences in projects like the new organic garden that started in 2015 and an initiative with the Engineering Department to restore Ti'at canoes. There have been other, less official influences as well. Alvitre said students living in the dorms near the twenty-two acres report hearing strange sounds at night that they swear sound like ghosts. "This university is unique," said Alvitre. "Cal State Long Beach is not UCLA, Cal State Long Beach is not Fullerton. It's not Harvard…we're on a sacred site, there's a different consciousness."

14

Football, Greek Housing and Historic Preservation

Big Ideas That Didn't Quite Make It

One could make the case that Long Beach State is more famous for killing its football team than for fielding one for thirty-seven seasons. It was one of a number of campus ideas that never quite caught on.

Football

Football started big but never seemed to capture the imagination of the campus. However, several players and fans will tell you it was good fun while it lasted. The first Forty-Niner team kicked off in 1955 amid the "let's put on a show" enthusiasm that launched a host of other sports and activities on campus in the '50s. Soon there was a marching band, which stepped out in the school colors of brown and gold. However, marching band director Dr. John Green said the brown faded too much, so he quietly changed the band uniforms to black and gold. This clashed with the school fight song that claimed, "Just like days of old, we'll fight Brown and Gold."

The football team loped along with about even won-loss records through the 1950s and '60s and attracted mostly modest crowds at Veterans Memorial Stadium, where most of the games were played. After one unexpected win in the early 1960s, a crowd of the faithful convoyed to the *Long Beach Independent Press-Telegram* office with the aim of serenading sports editor Hank Hollingworth, the wag who coined the phrase "hilltop mausoleum" to describe Long Beach State's lack of sports spirit. The crowd, smarting from the slur on its gridiron loyalty, gleefully vented in song:

How you do, Mr. Hollingworth, how do you do?
How you do, Mr. Hollingworth, how do you do?
Oh, you think you're social class, but you're just a horse's ass.
How do you do, Mr. Hollingworth, how do you doooooo?

On most Friday nights, about 2,000 to 4,000 typically filled the stands at Vets Stadium, which holds 11,600. Long Beach Polytechnic High School drew more.

Even football coach Jim Strangeland, among the most successful of Long Beach State coaches, raged to Hollingworth in a 1973 *Independent Press-Telegram* column about the fact that, generally speaking, a few thousand fans attended games every week: "It's aggravating to work your tail off to produce an exciting football team and then find nobody in the stands."

Hollingworth, who had made the same observation countless times, noted in the same space, "It was ever thus at Long Beach State, a school unfortunately noted for its glaring lack of support for its athletic teams, particularly its football squad."

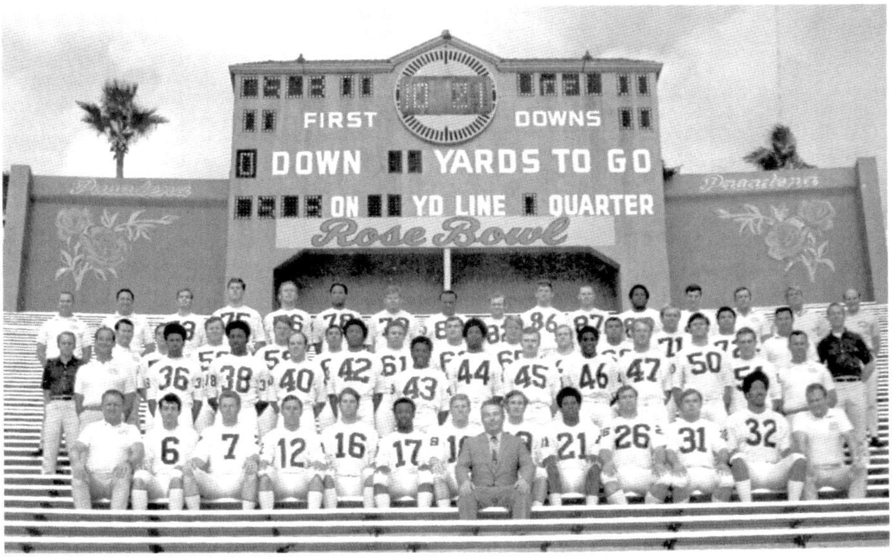

The 1970 squad at the Pasadena Bowl. The team landed its only bowl game by upsetting coach Don Coryell's San Diego State team 27–11 at Anaheim Stadium. *Courtesy of Long Beach State Athletics.*

The program produced some NFL veterans such as Terrell Davis, a relentless running back for the Denver Broncos. Another was future Long Beach councilman Dee Andrews, a running back who starred at Long Beach Polytechnic High School and Long Beach City College before breaking school rushing records at "State."

Probably the heyday of the football program came when Strangeland took over in 1969. The next year, the 49ers, after a brutal training session on Terminal Island, upset San Diego State, 27–11, and San Diego's "Air Coryell" passing attack, made famous by Coach Don Coryell. After the win, Long Beach State fans poured onto the Anaheim Stadium field. That led to the team's only bowl game. The 49ers tied Louisville, 24–24, in the Pasadena Bowl.

Three years later, the NCAA announced sanctions against Long Beach State's football and basketball programs for recruiting violations and improper gifts. Students and boosters were furious and claimed the violations were small and that bigger, better-funded programs were as culpable or worse. The three years of sanctions "brought the program to its knees," wrote Mike Guardabascio in his book *Football in Long Beach*.

President Steve Horn started talking about eliminating football in the 1970s and '80s, but alums and community members raised money to save it. The program was in decline when athletics officials tried a Hail Mary pass, hiring NFL legend George Allen to coach the team. The seventy-one-year-old was known for transforming the Washington Redskins and L.A. Rams from losers to winners, and he intended to do the same in Long Beach. Sportswriters were incredulous. "Why George?" read one *Sports Illustrated* headline. His family was shocked; he joked that his wife told him if he took the job, according to news accounts, she'd start smoking again.

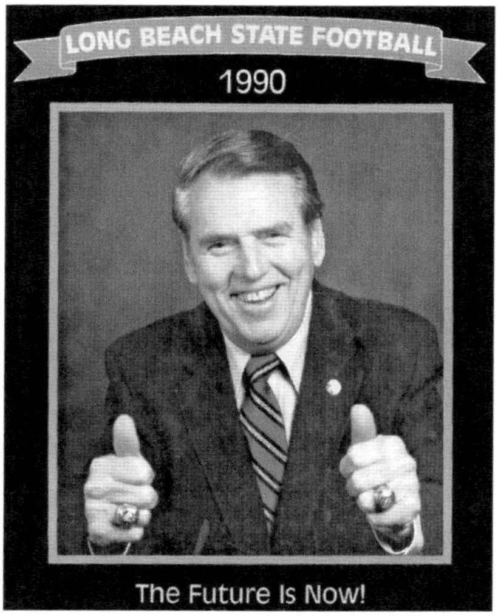

George Allen was going to provide the star power that would revive football, and he did, for one season. *Courtesy of Long Beach State Athletics.*

But the football-mad coach, who was taking over a team that was 11-24 for the last three years, swept into town with a hail of good will and a ton of publicity. One of the first things he did was declare that the team's colors would forever and anon be black and gold instead of brown and gold. (The fight song would remain unchanged.)

Allen, who never coached a losing season in the NFL, opened with a 59–0 loss against Clemson. But the team fought to a 6-5 record, its best mark since 1986. After squeaking out a win against UNLV for the last game, excited players threw a bucket of icy water on Allen at the end. He later joked that the school couldn't afford Gatorade. Allen got sick but recovered. However, by December 31, 1990, he was dead of a heart arrhythmia, or irregular heartbeat. Allen was seventy-two.

Allen's death stunned his players and sent the program, which was reeling before his arrival, into a tailspin. The marquee coach was gone, and with him went any serious talk of fundraising or a football comeback. Assistant Willie Brown, the former Oakland Raiders and Denver Broncos cornerback who would make it to the Hall of Fame, took over the team in 1991, and the 2-9 finish was its last. A university committee recommended ending the program, and the team was disbanded in December 1991.

Former history professor David Bernstein was on the committee that he said unanimously agreed to pull the plug. "It's a huge budget drain,"

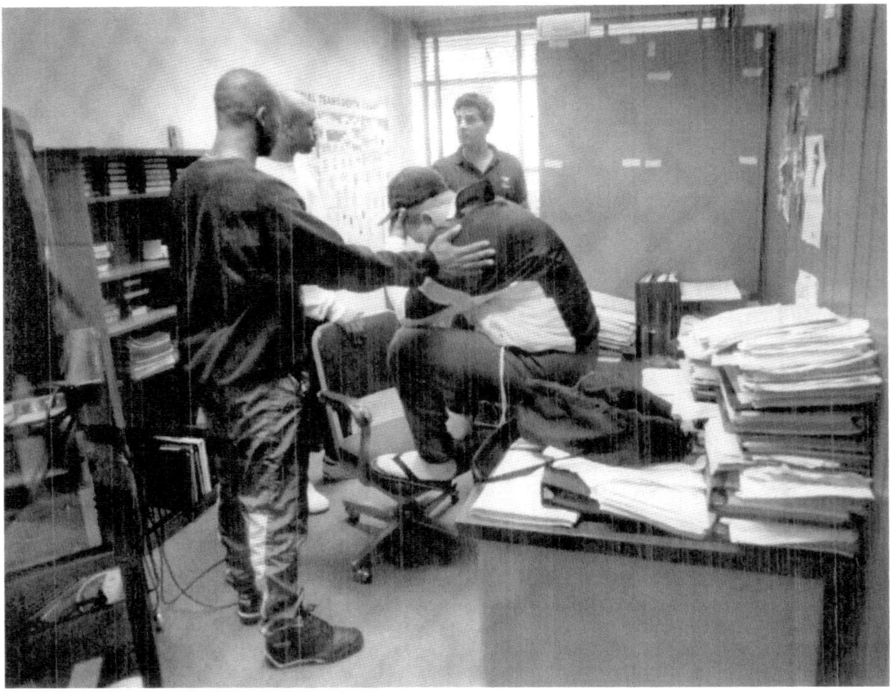

Players react to the December 1991 announcement that football at Long Beach State would end immediately. *Courtesy of the* Long Beach Press-Telegram.

Bernstein said. "Members of the community said, 'Don't do it, we can afford it, we'll raise the money'…They didn't come up with a penny."

The consistently low attendance; the "body bag" games against the bigger, better-funded programs; the expense; and the competition with USC and UCLA up the road all contributed to a pretty easy recommendation for President Curtis McCray. He accepted it. "It was a sad vote," said Bernstein. "We all wanted to save the program."

The campus community has made peace with the decision. Pretty much. "It was one of the biggest mistakes we ever made," said Perry Moore, who was the athletic director from 1974 to 1982 before taking a job as assistant vice-president of student affairs. "If we kept football, we would have been a different place as a university…we had a tremendous group of players and were ready to jump to the top when George Allen died."

It was a decision subsequent presidents supported. Alums to this day pepper campus fundraisers with questions about the return of football. While there have been short, heady bursts of interest to restart football, they invariably die out. Even sports-loving former president F. King Alexander dismissed the idea as just too expensive. President Jane Close Conoley, in 2015, also said no way.

The legacy of those years remains in the George Allen Field on lower campus, which plays host mostly to soccer and, in the summer, children's camps. Then there are the shirts that read, "Long Beach State Football, Undefeated Since 1991." Those $16.95 souvenirs are still one of the biggest sellers at the bookstore.

Greek Housing on Campus

About 10 percent of students on the Long Beach State campus are members of fraternities or sororities. In the 1950s and '60s, Greek life was the engine that drove the campus social scene, creating Forty-Niner Days, Hello Days, Spring Sing and other activities that welcomed new students to an unknown college.

Back then, planners carved out a place for fraternity and sorority houses on the emerging campus. Ellie Johnson, the daughter of the first president, P. Victor Peterson, recalled talk of turning part of Beach Drive near Atherton into a small Greek row. An early 1960s master plan showed a line of "communal housing" structures along Atherton Street.

Indeed, authors of the 1963 master plan for the campus wagged their fingers at campus officials, saying Greek housing needed to be put on campus as city officials had little interest in seeing a Greek row among the residential houses of Long Beach:

> *The City authorities are adamant that this housing must be located within the confines of the College site. The property for the College was originally given to the State by the City of Long Beach and it has always been the intention of the City that the fraternities and sororities should be located here. This has been repeatedly pointed out by the refusal of the City to allow zoning for this housing other than on the college site.*

Today, fraternity and sorority houses are scattered throughout Long Beach—tucked between Craftsman houses, convenience stores and beauty parlors. Students must placate noise-averse neighbors with notes alerting them to potential parties. A *Forty-Niner* editorial in 1969 criticized the city for using a 1906 housing ordinance to evict residents of a fraternity house, part of what it called a campaign to "purge" Greeks from residential areas.

In recent years, journalism graduate Lauren Weiss's Sigma Kappa house was tucked up in a gated community in Signal Hill. It was quiet and safe, and the women liked that. But it was a good thing Weiss specialized in public relations. "Neighbors would get frustrated when we had a meeting or philanthropy event," said Weiss, who does marketing and event planning for an Orange County magazine. "We try to be polite and send a letter out to neighbors weeks in advance. 'Here's the president's number for questions or concerns.' We do everything we can to work with them. It's not perfect all the time."

So what happened? Why didn't campus officials listen to the master planners and city officials? In the 1960s, the lawyers at the new CSU system killed the Greeks-on-campus notion because they thought it would never fly with the state of California. That's because fraternities and sororities are, by their nature, exclusionary, and legal counsel felt such enterprises would not be able to get state funding.

Around the early 2000s, the idea to create Greek housing on campus was floated anew, but nothing came of it. At one time, the university explored a plan to buy a piece of land near the Los Cerritos Wetlands close to Second Street and Pacific Coast Highway for Greek housing. However, the project never went anywhere, in part because it was so close to the difficult-to-develop wetlands.

Rosemary Taylor Schmidt, the 1964 graduate and later activities director, said she recalls "talk and promises" to Greek students and alumni about housing on campus but nothing really getting done. Brett Waterfield, the director of student life and development, said there has been talk of inviting Greek houses on campus. "We had conversations about it when [President Robert] Maxson was here. One of the issues that came up was the campus policies and the fact that it's a dry campus. All of a sudden the room gets real quiet."

President Jane Close Conoley said she would love to get the Greek community on campus some day. "Students are safer on campus, more engaged and more likely to graduate...It's on my long-term wish list. I think everybody would be safer." But it would be a choice for the sororities and fraternities, some of which own their own houses. "If they were on campus, we would have more control."

Historic Preservation

In 1970, President Stephen Horn launched the university oral history program when the college was twenty-one years old. He eventually recruited Sherna Berger Gluck, who was working on a project to interview local Rosie the Riveters who spent World War II working in local aircraft factories. Gluck launched a program to train interviewers and select narrators. Soon, historians were interviewing the first campus officials, faculty and students and even Horn himself.

The campus historians collected a rich trove of historical perspective on the university's formative years. Some were lost as old tapes deteriorated. However, scores of interviews live on in the University Archives as digital files or written transcripts. Several interviews were put online in a digital repository, allowing anyone with computer access to hear from those who were on campus when the university began.

The first campus buildings, however, did not fare quite as well. The original Park Estates apartments that housed the college in its infancy stood until the 1980s, when most of them were knocked down to make way for new apartment units.

One of the original buildings was trucked over to the new campus. It was tiny, ten by ten feet. It was once a bookstore and the first student government office. In the 1970s, campus officials moved the tiny building to the area where the College of Business Administration is now. There were tennis courts nearby at the time, and the Athletic Department used it to store

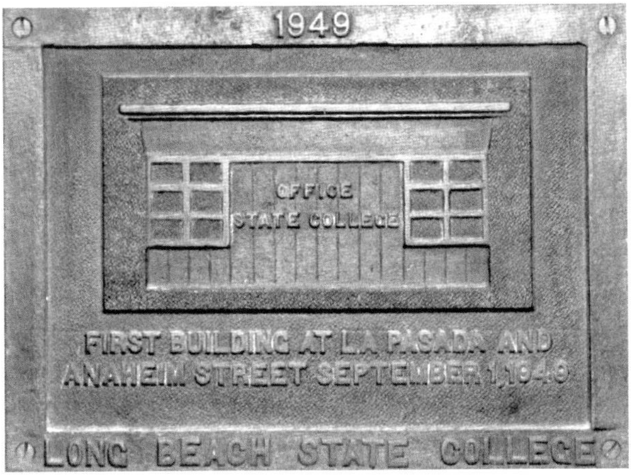

Left: The university placed a plaque on one of the remaining buildings from the original apartments, and then someone ran off with it and probably melted it down. *Courtesy of the University Archives.*

Below: Almost all the original Park Estates apartments were demolished and rebuilt in the 1980s. *Courtesy of the University Archives.*

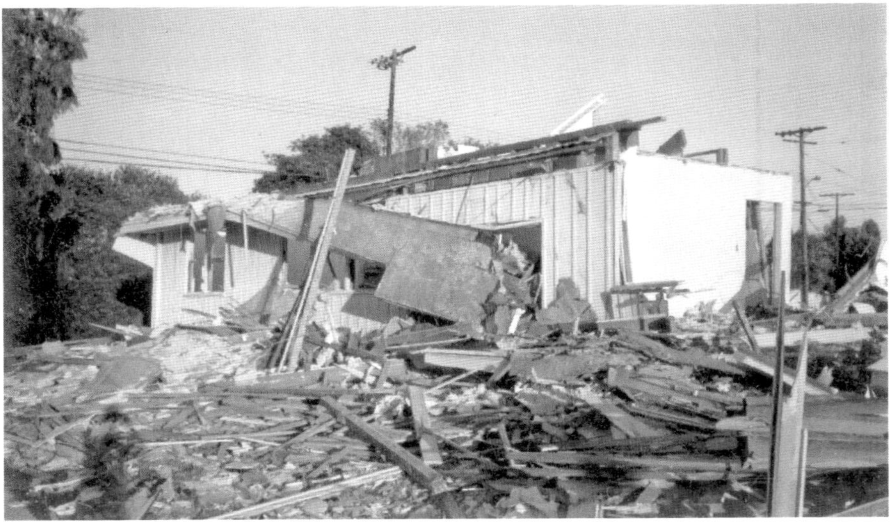

equipment. The plan was to eventually set up a historic area with a plaque to mark one of the original buildings of the nascent Long Beach State campus.

But in the late 1970s, the plaque disappeared—stolen and likely melted down as scrap metal, said former physical planning and facilities director Jon Regnier. Some days later, the house, which was resting on a concrete slab, was gone, too, carted away by thieves for its full-sized, good-quality redwood two-by-fours. With it went the last physical presence of the college's simple, halcyon beginnings.

15

The Famous

"Pointy Birds, oh Pointy, Pointy"

Comedian and actor Steve Martin's banjo playing won the Sigma Pi hootenanny in 1964. He broke into television in 1966 when a friend recommended him to Stu Rosen, a recent Long Beach State grad who was producing a children's TV show in L.A. called *Dusty's Attic*. Rosen, who would go on to win several daytime Emmys, needed a banjo player. Martin was then working on his magic act at Knott's Berry Farm.

They met at Rosen's parents' house in Park Estates. Rosen recalled that Martin showed up for the first shoot with a fever, but he did the show. "He was funny. He was great," Rosen said.

Martin went on to write for the *Smothers Brothers Comedy Hour*. The next time Rosen spoke with Martin, in the mid-1970s, Martin told him, "I'm not going to write anymore, I'm going to go on the road for myself, and I'm going to play all the toilets in the country" to get experience.

The Garden Grove resident had studied philosophy for three years at Long Beach State before he transferred to UCLA for theater. Martin didn't graduate from either institution, but in 1989, Long Beach State handed Martin its first honorary doctorate, in humanities. During the August ceremony, the comedian—known for his movies, stand-up act and *Saturday Night Live* King Tut number—mused about which one of his esteemed works earned him the honorary.

Wearing a black cap and gown and doctoral hood, Martin recited his lyrics from the famous number, ending "Born in Arizona, moved to Babylonia/Born in Arizona, got a condo made of stone-a, King Tut."

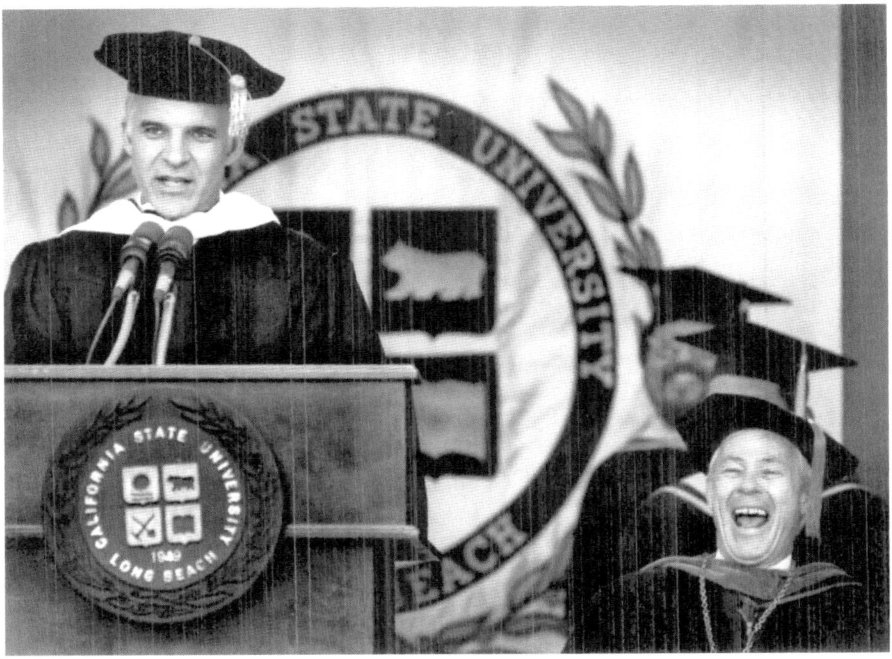

Steve Martin receives his honorary doctorate in humanities in August 1989. He recited the lines from *King Tut* and *The Man with Two Brains* and cracked up a crowd of about three thousand, including new president Curtis McCray. *Courtesy of* Long Beach Press-Telegram.

Next, he recited poetry from his films *The Man with Two Brains* and *L.A. Story*, "Pointy birds, oh pointy, pointy. Anoint my head, anointy-nointy."

Then, he turned to newly inaugurated president Curtis McCray, who held a PhD in English, and said, "I'm sure you're sorry you took up Chaucer now."

Fellow students Richard and Karen Carpenter of Downey were on their way to pop superstardom when they gave Martin his big break when they booked him as their opening act, according to the *Press-Telegram*. Richard played piano, and Karen played drums and had to be coaxed to stand up on stage and sing. She did, with what *Rolling Stone* called her "chocolate and cream alto voice."

The Carpenters sang in the choir directed by the legendary Frank Pooler, the handsome, turtleneck-sporting choral impresario who shaped the university choirs when he came to the college in the late 1950s. Pooler, who was educated at St. Olaf College in Minnesota, expected punctuality and professionalism, and he cared deeply about his students.

Pooler nurtured the Carpenters, encouraging them to try a blended sound, which they used to gold record effect with "We've Only Just Begun"

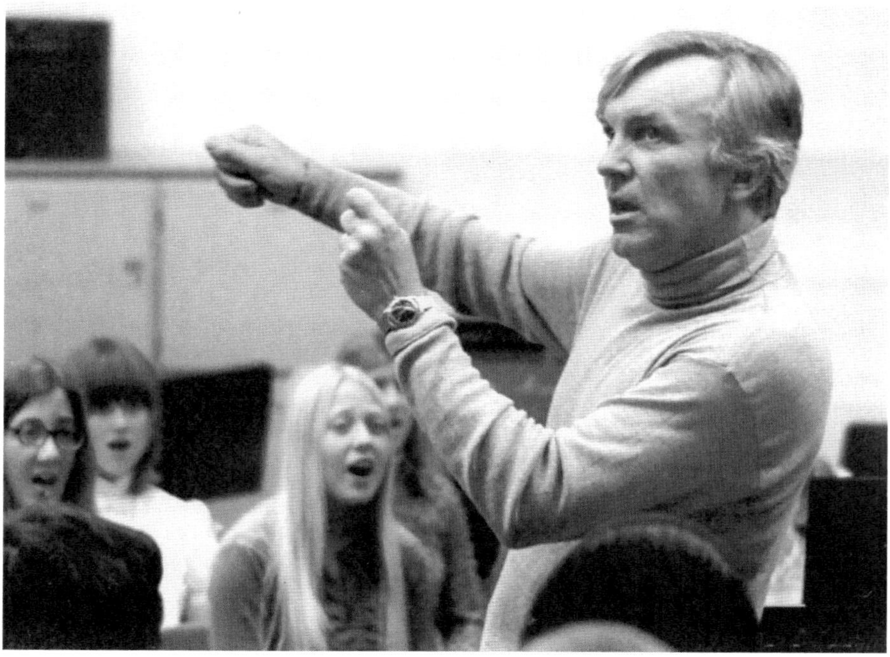

Frank Pooler, who was schooled at St. Olaf College in Minnesota, brought the Long Beach State music program to a higher level.

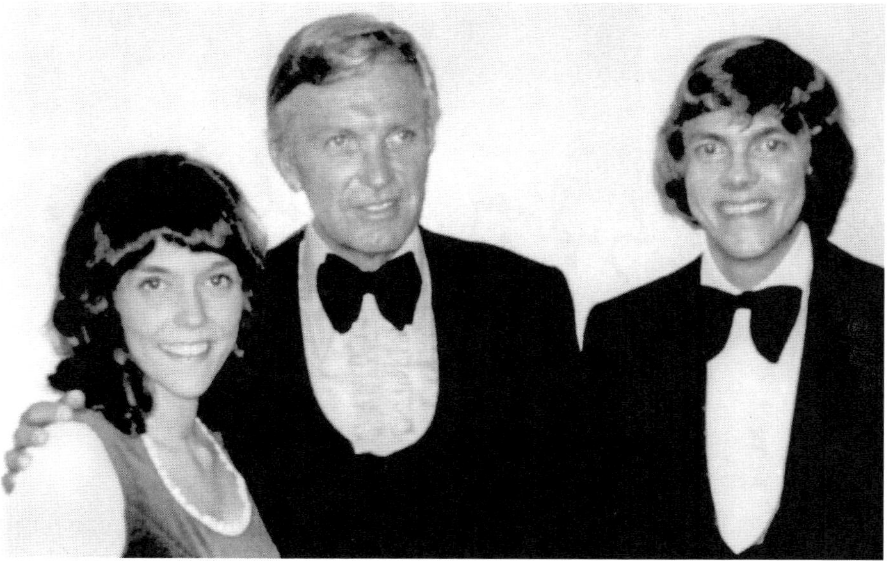

Long Beach State choir director Frank Pooler mentored the Carpenters and influenced their smooth sound, which was different from a lot of popular music in the 1960s. *Courtesy of CSULB.*

and "Superstar." Pooler also co-wrote "Merry Christmas Darling" with Richard Carpenter. The Carpenters performed in the Gold Mine gym as well as the Terrace Theater in Long Beach in 1978, which was Karen's final performance. Karen died in 1983. The Long Beach State choir sang at her funeral at a Downey church.

••• • •••

A botched renovation to a campus baseball field contributed to the savoir-faire of a team that helped bring a parade of soon-to-be-famous athletes through campus. In the late 1980s, the baseball team had to look elsewhere for games and practices. The assistant coach, Dave Malpas, took the team to the Pony League field at nearby Whaley Park, which then was dusty and dirty and not much better than the rocky campus field.

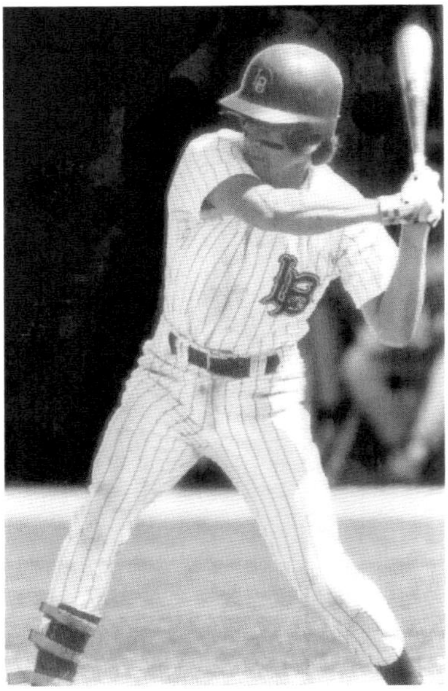

Jason Giambi, one of the early Dirtbags and later an American League MVP, at bat in the early 1990s. *Courtesy of Long Beach State Athletics.*

"Part of the thing about going over there was to develop some mental toughness and take ground balls on an all-dirt field," recalled former coach Dave Snow, now a player development consultant with the San Diego Padres. One day the assistant coach brought the players back from a workout "sweating dirt from top to bottom. I made a comment, 'You look like a bunch of dirtbags, and that's kinda what we are.'"

Under Snow, it became a badge of honor to get filthy diving for every ball and sliding for every base. In Snow's first year, the team went from winning fourteen games in 1988 to fifty in 1989. An Athletics Department marketing guru made the unofficial name official in 1993, when the team moved to Blair Field by Wilson High School.

Players who came through Snow's program included Jason Giambi and Chris Gomez. Later on, Gold Glove winners Evan Longoria and Troy Tulowitzky and All-Star pitcher Jered Weaver were Dirtbags who started their million-dollar livelihoods at Long Beach State.

• • • ● • • •

Steven Spielberg was a student in the mid-1960s; he left after three years when he got a job in the movie industry. Spielberg—the director of *Schindler's List*, *Jaws* and *E.T.*—returned in 2001 to finish the bachelor's degree work he started. Registering under an assumed name known to only a handful of faculty, he submitted the Oscar-winning *Schindler's List* to pass advanced filmmaking. Spielberg also filed a paper to complete his general education requirement, according to a 2002 article in the *Los Angeles Times*. Spielberg walked with a bodyguard and thousands of other undergrads for the May 31, 2002 ceremony. President Robert Maxson told the media then that Spielberg wanted his children to know he got his degree—in his case, thirty-seven years later.

• • • ● • • •

One of the students in journalism professor Larry Meyer's contemporary magazine class was a "devilishly handsome, blond surfer type" who commanded the full attention of his female classmates, Meyer recalled. "I thought, 'Oh boy, here we go,'" Meyer said of the student with the megawatt smile who also wrote for a surf magazine. "He was a pretty boy with a pretty face, but damned if he wasn't really sharp. He spoke up in class…really a bright guy."

That guy, 1979 journalism graduate Chris Carter, went to Hollywood to write for movies and eventually created the popular sci-fi TV drama *The X-Files*. When Meyer got word his star student was making it in Hollywood, he said he wasn't surprised. "He was a gifted fellow, very modest and polite." Meyer added he was in his first year of teaching when he met Carter. "I see I rushed to conclusions."

• • • ● • • •

When Congressman Dana Rohrabacher arrived on campus in the mid-1960s, the Republican immediately became immersed in the fight against Communism, even flying to Vietnam and spending Christmas vacation in Prague, Czechoslovakia. Rohrabacher, a Republican, said he enjoyed arguing in front of the bookstore with liberal students who were quoting Marx and Lenin. He said he respected his more leftist fellow students and said the spirited discussions helped hone his own political skills.

The 1969 history graduate does have one regret, though. "I missed out on a lot of great socializing by being too politically active," he says now. "By senior year, I did have a couple fine girlfriends I liked a lot. But I would have spent more time in Hussongs in Baja rather than Prague and Vietnam. I was out trying to save the world; I should have been involved more with socializing and revelry."

APPENDIX 1

List of Presidents

P. Victor Peterson, July 1949–June 1959
  Interim: Henry Magnuson, July–August 1959
Carl McIntosh, September 1959–February 1969
  Acting: Donald H. Simonsen, February–July 1970
Stephen Horn, August 1970–February 1988
  Acting: June Cooper, February–May 1988
Curtis McCray, May 1988–January 1993
  Interim: Karl Anatol, January 1993–May 1994
Robert Maxson, June 1994–January 2006
F. King Alexander, January 2006–June 2013
  Interim: Donald Para, July 2013–June 2014
Jane Close Conoley, July 2014–present

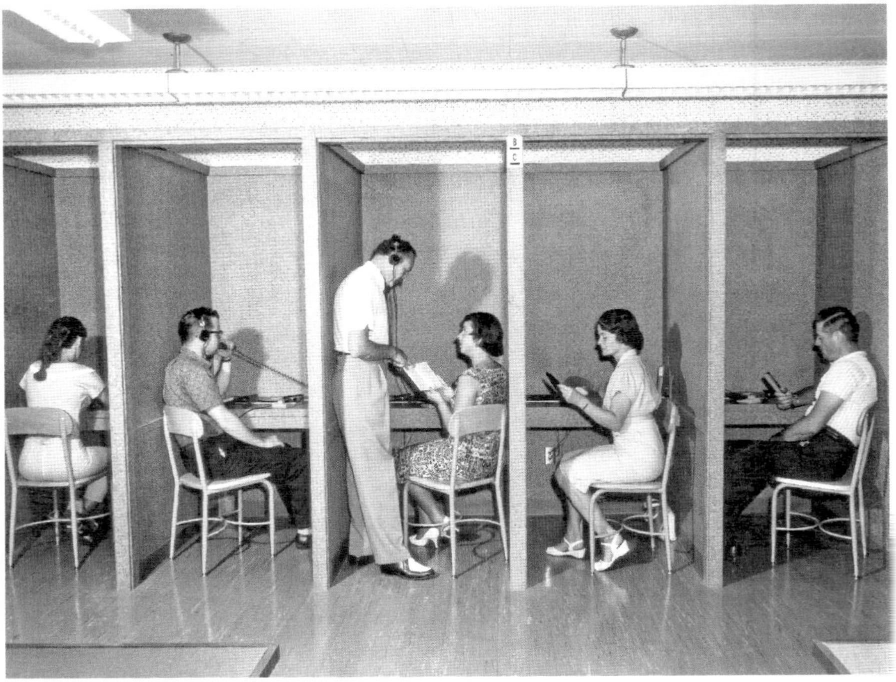

An early 1960s language lab. *Courtesy of the University Archives.*

APPENDIX 2

University Buildings and Dates Built

University Building	Date Built
Liberal Arts 3	1954
Liberal Arts 2	1954
KKJZ building	1954
Fine Arts 1	1954
Fine Arts 2	1954
University Theatre	1955
Liberal Arts 4	1955
Lecture Hall 150–151	1955
Peterson Hall 2	1956
Faculty Office 2	1957
Education 1	1957
University Telecommunication Center	1958
Fine Arts 3	1958
Kinesiology	1958
Peterson Hall 1	1959
Academic Services	1959

UNIVERSITY BUILDING	DATE BUILT
Los Alamitos Hall	1959
Los Cerritos Hall	1959
Liberal Arts 5	1959
Cafeteria	1960
Design	1960
Education 2	1961
Soroptimist House	1962
Electrical Substation N	1962
Fine Arts 4	1962
Engineering 2	1962
Engineering 3	1962
Engineering 4	1962
Liberal arts 1	1962
Health and Human Services	1965
Health and Human Services 2	1965
Human Services and Design	1966
McIntosh Humanities Building	1967
Language Arts	1967
Greenhouse 3	1969
Nursing	1969
Faculty Office 4	1969
Faculty Office 5	1969
Family and Consumer Science	1970
Art Annex	1970
Psychology	1970
Library	1971

Appendix 2

University Building	Date Built
Multimedia Center	1971
Vivian Engineering Center	1971
Studio Theater	1972
University Student Union	1972
Electrical Substation S	1972
Patterson Child Devlopment Center	1975
E. James Brotman Hall	1975
Bookstore	1975
Student Health Services	1976
Social Science/Public Affairs	1976
Engineering Technology	1977
Recycling Center	1977
Facilities Management	1978
Microbiology	1979
Corporation Yard	1979
Outpost	1979
University Music Center	1982
Residence Hall A	1983
Residence Hall B	1983
Residence Hall C	1983
Residence Hall D	1983
Residence Hall E	1983
Residence Hall F	1983
Residence Hall G	1983
Residence Hall H	1983
Residence Hall I	1983

UNIVERSITY BUILDING	DATE BUILT
Residence Hall J/Commons	1983
Residence Hall K	1983
Residence Hall L	1983
Residence Hall M	1983
Residence Hall N	1983
Residence Hall P	1983
Residence Hall Q	1983
Residence Hall R	1983
Residence Hall S	1983
Residence Hall T	1983
Residence Hall U	1983
Residence Hall V	1983
International House	1987
Engineering/Computer Science	1989
Housing and Residential Life	1989
Earl Burns Miller Garden	1990
Miller House	1992
Steve and Nini Horn Center	1993
Visitor Information	1993
Carpenter Performing Arts Center	1993
Faculty Office 3	1993
Business Administration	1993
Walter Pyramid	1994
Parking Structure 1	1995
Central Plant	1997
University Police Building	2002

UNIVERSITY BUILDING	DATE BUILT
Molecular and Life Science	2003
Neil and Phyllis Barrett Athletic Administration Center	2004
Parking Structure 2	2006
Parking Structure 3	2008
Student Recreation Center	2010
Hall of Science	2011

Source: Physical Planning and Facilities Management

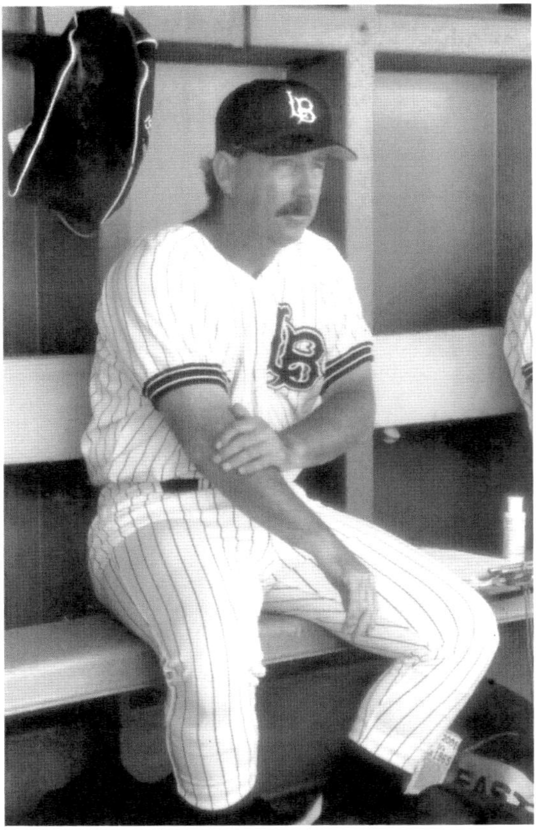

Dirtbag coach Dave Snow in the dugout in the 1990s.
Courtesy of Long Beach State Athletics.

APPENDIX 3

Coaches and Team Records

Selected Sports

Baseball

Name	Years	Record	Conference Titles	NCAA Tournament Appearances	NCAA Titles
John McConnell	1954–59 (6)	86-65 (.570)	none	none	none
Dick Clegg	1960–63 (4)	52-79-1 (.397)	none	none	none
Bob Wuesthoff	1964–69 (6)	161-101-4 (.615)	2 (1964, 1969)	1 (1964)	none
John Gonsalves	1970–88 (19)	462-634-16 (.422)	1 (1970)	1 (1970)	none
Dave Snow	1989–2001 (13)	511-290-4 (.637)	6 (1989, 1992–94, 1996, 1998)	11 (1989, 1991–99, 2001)	4 College World Series appearances (1989, 1991, 1993, 1998)

Name	Years	Record	Conference Titles	NCAA Tournament Appearances	NCAA Titles
Mike Weathers	2002–10 (9)	311-213 (.593)	2 (2003, 2008)	6 (2002–05, 20007–08)	none
Troy Buckley	2011–present (4)	120-107 (.528)	none	1 (2014)	none

Men's Basketball

Name	Years	Record	Conference Titles	NCAA Tournament Appearances	NCAA Titles
Herm Schwarzkopf	1950–52 (2)	13-27 (.325)	none	none	none
Earl Kidd	1952–57 (5)	48-71 (.403)	none	none	none
Bill Patterson	1957–60 (3)	37-33 (.529)	none	none	none
Dick Perry	1960–67 (7)	82-96 (.491)	none	none	none
Randy Sandefur	1967–68 (1)	12-13 (.480)	none	none	none
Jerry Tarkanian	1968–73 (5)	122-20 (.859)	4 (1969–73)	4 (1969–73); 2 Elite 8 (1971–72) and 2 Sweet 16 (1970, 1973)	none
Lute Olson	1973–74 (1)	24-2 (.923)	1 (1974)	none	none
Dwight Jones	1974–78 (4)	70-40 (.636)	3 (1974–77)	1 (1977)	none

Name	Years	Record	Conference Titles	NCAA Tournament Appearances	NCAA Titles
Tex Winter	1978–83 (5)	78-69 (.531)	none	1 NIT (1980)	none
Dave Buss	1983–84 (1)	9-19 (.321)	none	None	none
Ron Palmer	1984–87 (3)	23-64 (.264)	none	None	none
Joe Harrington	1987–90 (3)	53-36 (.596)	none	2 NIT (1988, 1990)	none
Seth Greenberg	1990–96 (6)	105-70 (.600)	none	2 NCAA (1993, 95) 1 NIT (1992)	none
Wayne Morgan	1996–2002 (6)	91-84 (.520)	none	1 NIT (2000)	none
Larry Reynolds	2002–07 (5)	63-83 (.432)	1 (2007)	1 (2007)	none
Dan Monson	2008–present (8)	135-125 (.519)	3 (2011, 2012, 2013)	1 (2012)	none

Women's Basketball

Name	Years	Record	Conference Titles	NCAA Tournament Appearances	NCAA Titles
Fran Schaafsma	1962–79 (17)	208-73 (.740)	11 (1965–76)	5 (73, 76-79) AIAW	none
Joan Bonvicini	1979-91 (12)	325-71 (.821)	10 (1980–82, 1984–89, 1991)	2 AIAW (1979–80) 10 NCAA (1982–91)	2 Final Fours (1987, 1988)

NAME	YEARS	RECORD	CONFERENCE TITLES	NCAA TOURNAMENT APPEARANCES	NCAA TITLES
Glenn McDonald	1991–95 (4)	54-58 (.482)	none	1 (1992)	none
Dalla Bolla	1995–2003 (8)	120-112 (.517)	none	1 WNIT (2000)	none
Mary Hegarty	2003–08 (6)	70-99 (.438)	1 (2006)	none	none
Jody Wynn	2009–present (5)	90-99 (.476)	none	none	none

FOOTBALL

NAME	YEARS	RECORD	CONFERENCE TITLES	NCAA TOURNAMENT APPEARANCES	NCAA TITLES
Mike DeLotto	1955–57 (3)	13-10-0 (.565)	none	none	none
Don Reed	1958–68 (11)	57-47-2 (.548)	none	none	none
Jim Strangeland	1969–73 (5)	31-24-2 (.564)	2 (1970–71)	1 (1970)	none
Wayne Howard	1974–76 (3)	23-10-0 (.697)	none	none	none
Dave Currey	1977–83 (7)	40-36-0 (.526)	1 (1980)	none	none
Mike Sheppard	1984–86 (3)	16-18-0 (.471)	none	none	none
Larry Reisbig	1987–89 (3)	11-24-0 (.314)	none	none	none

Name	Years	Record	Conference Titles	NCAA Tournament Appearances	NCAA Titles
George Allen	1990 (1)	6-5-0 (.545)	none	none	none
Willie Brown	1991 (1)	2-9-0 (.182)	none	none	none

Men's Tennis

Name	Years	Record	Conference Titles	NCAA Tournament Appearances	NCAA Titles
Bob Stichter	1951–52 (1)	N/A	N/A	N/A	none
Earl Kidd	1952–55, 1960-62 (5)	N/A	N/A	N/A	none
Bob Pestolesi	1955–60, 1962–63 (6)	N/A	N/A	N/A	none
Dan Campbell	1963–75, 1976–84 (20)	N/A	4 (1973–74, 1982, 1984)	N/A	none
Kurt Nielson	1975–76 (1)	N/A	1 (1976)	N/A	none
Larry Easley	1984–87 (3)	N/A	1 (1986)	1 (1987)	none
Peter Smith	1987–91 (4)	N/A	none	none	none

Appendix 3

Women's Tennis

Name	Years	Record	Conference Titles	NCAA Tournament Appearances	NCAA Titles
Dorthy Deatherage	1964–65 (1)	N/A	N/A	N/A	none
Joan Mathews	1965–66 (1.5)	N/A	N/A	N/A	none
Lynne Riddle	1967–68 (1.5)	N/A	N/A	N/A	none
Ann Heck	1968–71 (3)	N/A	N/A	N/A	none
Carol Luther	1972–74 (2)	N/A	N/A	N/A	none
Gloria Hendricks	1974–76 (2)	N/A	N/A	N/A	none
Robin Kahn	1976–89 (13)	117-173 (.403)	N/A (record from 1980 on)	N/A	none
Michelle Archuleta	1989–93 (4)	24-80 (.231)	none	none	none
Jami Jones	1993–97 (4)	55-47-1 (.539)	none	none	none
Jenny Hilt-Costello	1997–present (18)	316-136 (.699)	11 (2002, 2004–09, 2011–12, 2014–15)	11 (2002, 2004–06, 2008–09, 2011–15)	none

Women's Soccer

Name	Years	Record	Conference Titles	NCAA Tournament Appearances	NCAA Titles
Rene Bohne	1983 (1)	7-6-5 (.527)	none	none	none
Ben Diaz	1984 (1)	12-9-0 (.571)	none	none	none
Larry Hanks	1985 (1)	12-4-3 (.711)	none	none	none
Graham Carr	1986 (1)	10-7-2 (.579)	independent	none	none
Julie Cochran	1998–2000 (3)	23-32-3 (.422)	none	none	none
Peter Reynaud	2001–03 (3)	19-29-5 (.405)	none	none	none
Mauricio Ingrassia	2004–present (11)	124-76-26 (.606)	3 (2006-2008)	4 (2008, 2010–12)	none

Softball

Name	Years	Record	Conference Titles	NCAA Tournament Appearances	NCAA Titles
Chris Miner	1981 (1)	8-24-0 (.250)	none	none	none
George Parris	1982–83 (2)	41-92-2 (.308)	none	none	none

Name	Years	Record	Conference Titles	NCAA Tournament Appearances	NCAA Titles
Pete Manarino	1984–2006 (23)	843-508-2 (.624)	5 (1996–97, 1999, 2004–05)	17 (1986–93, 1996–2000, 2003–06)	5 CWS (1986, 1990–93)
Kim Sowder	2007–present (9)	300-195 (.606)	3 (2008, 2012, 2014)	5 (2008–09, 2011–12, 2014)	none

Men's Volleyball

Name	Years	Record	Conference Titles	NCAA Tournament Appearances	NCAA Titles
Randy Sandefur	1970–74 (5)	35-29 (.547)	1 (1973)	4 (1970–73)	2nd (1970, 1973)
Miles Pabst	1975–76 (2)	7-17 (.292)	none	none	none
Dick Montgomery	1977–80 (4)	52-32 (.619)	none	1 (1978)	none
Don Paris	1981 (1)	15-13 (.536)	none	1 (1981)	none
Ray Ratelle	1982–2000 (19)	385-190 (.670)	6 (1973) (Division Winners: 1990, 1992, 1999–2001)	5 (1983–84, 1990–91, 1999)	1st (1991) 2nd (1990, 1999)
Alan Knipe	2001–2009 (9)	169-103 (.621)	1 (2008)	2 (2004, 2008)	2nd (2004)

Name	Years	Record	Conference Titles	NCAA Tournament Appearances	NCAA Titles
Andy Read (Interim)	2010–2012 (Interim) (3)	42-46 (.477)	none	none	none
Alan Knipe	2001–09, 2013–present (11)	211-121 (.635)	1 (2008)	2 (2004, 2008)	2nd (2004)

Sand Volleyball

Name	Years	Record	Conference Titles	NCAA Tournament Appearances	NCAA Titles
Brian Gimmillaro	2012 (1)	8-6 (.571)	none	1-AVCA (2012)	2nd AVCA (2012)
Matt Ulmer	2013 (1)	20-3 (.870)	none	1-AVCA (2013)	1st AVCA (2013)
Erika Dillard	2014–present (1)	10-5 (.667)	none	none	none

Women's Volleyball

Name	Years	Record	Conference Titles	NCAA Tournament Appearances	NCAA Titles
Fran Schaafsma	1964–70 (7)	68-21 (.773)	unknown	2 AIAW (1969–70)	2nd (1970)

NAME	YEARS	RECORD	CONFERENCE TITLES	NCAA TOURNAMENT APPEARANCES	NCAA TITLES
Ann Heck	1971 (1)	28-5 (.849)	unknown	1 AIAW (1971)	2nd (1971)
Dixie Grimmett	1972–84 (13)	250-169-6 (.597)	unknown	8 AIAW (1972–79)	1st (1972) 1st (1973) (AIAW)
Brian Gimmillaro	1985–present (30)	789-205 (.793)	13 (1991–94, 1996–98, 2001, 2005, 2008–09, 2011, 2014)	27 (1985, 1987–2011, 2014)	1st (1989, 1993, 1998) 2nd (1991, 2001)

MEN'S WATER POLO

NAME	YEARS	RECORD	CONFERENCE TITLES	NCAA TOURNAMENT APPEARANCES	NCAA TITLES
Gordon Warner	1956 (1)	N/A	N/A	N/A	none
Herb Devries	1957–61 (4)	46-13 (.789)	N/A	N/A	none
Jim Schultz	1961–74 (14)	N/A	1 (1970) [records prior to 1970 unavailable]	4 (1969–71, 1973)	none
Ken Lindgren	1975–98 (24)	335-338-3 (.497)	5(1975, 1981, 1983, 1988–89)	7(1975, 1981, 1983, 1985, 1988–89, 1991)	2nd (1981)
Ricardo Azevedo	1999–2005 (7)	107-96 (.527)	none	none	none

NAME	YEARS	RECORD	CONFERENCE TITLES	NCAA TOURNAMENT APPEARANCES	NCAA TITLES
Gavin Arroyo	2006–present (9)	140-106 (.569)	none	none	none

WOMEN'S WATER POLO

NAME	YEARS	RECORD	CONFERENCE TITLES	NCAA TOURNAMENT APPEARANCES	NCAA TITLES
Sandy Vesser-Schneider	1998–99 (2)	19-47 (.288)	none	none	none
Ricardo Azevedo	2000–05 (6)	119-75 (.613)	none	none	none
Ken Lindgren	2006 (1)	15-14 (.517)	none	none	none
Catharine von Schwarz	2007–08 (2)	24-36 (.400)	none	none	none
Gavin Arroyo	2009–present (7)	103-108 (.488)	none	none	none

Source: Long Beach State Athletics

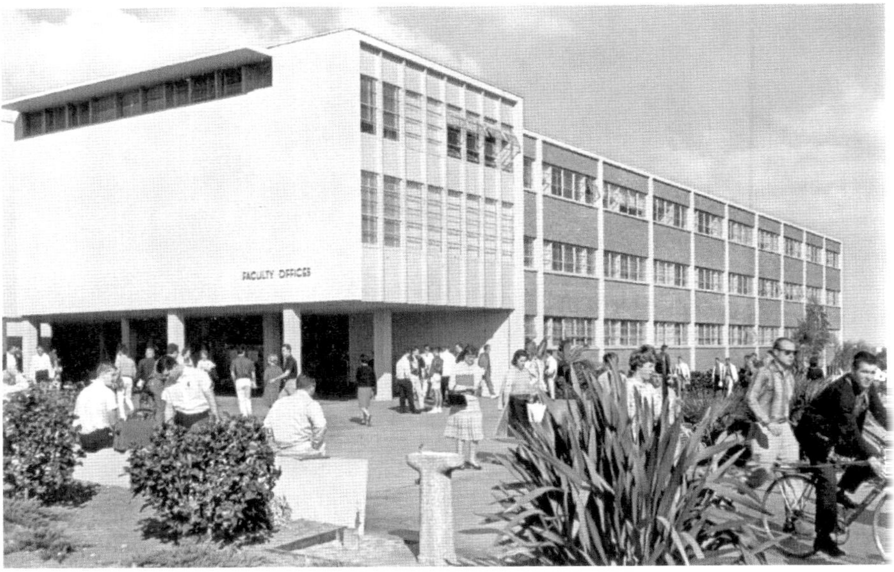

A 1960s Long Beach State postcard photo from in front of the faculty office building. *Courtesy of the CSULB Archives.*

Bibliography

Information in these chapters comes from oral histories and live interviews, as well as the documents noted here. Other sources are noted in the text.

Interviews

1. No Buildings, No Books

Irving Ahlquist, interviewed by Sherna Berger Gluck, December 13, 1977, CSULB University Library Digital Depository, Virtual Oral/Aural History Archive.

Memorandum from University Library Director Charles Boorkman, CSULB University Archives, December 3, 1973.

Beverly O'Neill, interview with the author, May 25, 2014.

Isabel Patterson, interview by Cindy Cleary, February 7, 1979, CSULB University Library Digital Depository, Virtual Oral/Aural History Archive.

Richard Wilde, interview by Kaye Briegel, November 11, 1980, CSULB University Library Digital Depository, Virtual Oral/Aural History Archive.

2. The Story of Long Beach State

Ellie Johnson, interview with the author, May 1, 2014.

P. Victor Peterson, former assemblyman William Grant and Don Gill of the CSULB Foundation, interviewed by Stephen Horn, February 25, 1971, transcript provided by the Peterson family.

P. Victor Peterson, handwritten notes on college founding, provided by the Peterson family.

3. P. Victor Peterson

Kaye Briegel, interview with the author, July 2014.

Lee Brown, interview with the author, March 31, 2014.

Francis "Frenchy" Flynn, interview by Gene Asher, August 11, 1978, transcript, CSULB Archives.

Ellie Johnson, interview with the author, May 1, 2014; August 1, 2014.

Bill O'Neill, interview by Kaye Briegel, January 22, 1981, CSULB University Library Digital Depository, Virtual Oral/Aural History Archive.

P. Victor Peterson, former assemblyman William Grant and Don Gill of the CSULB Foundation, interviewed by Stephen Horn, February 25, 1971, transcript, provided by the Peterson family.

Richard Wilde, "A Fortunate Life: Autobiography of Richard Herbert Wilde," CSULB Archives, unpublished.

Richard Wilde, interview by Kaye Briegel, November 21, 1980, CSULB University Library Digital Depository, Virtual Oral/Aural History Archive.

4. Parking

Lee Brown, interview with the author, March 31, 2014.

Beverly O'Neill, interview with the author, May 25, 2014.

Dana Rohrabacher, interview with the author, March 21, 2015.

John Stacy, interview with the author, October, 26, 2014.

Bill Tilney, interview with the author, January 20, 2015.

5. The Campus

Bernstein and Briegel, "California State University."
Scott Charmack, interview with the author, January 4, 2015.
Francis "Frenchy" Flynn, interview by Gene Asher, August 11, 1978, transcript, CSULB Archives.
Raymond Lindgren, interview by Kaye Briegel, March 23, 1981, CSULB University Library Digital Depository, Virtual/Oral/Aural History Archive.
Edward Lovell, interview by Ann Andriesse, July 6, 1998, CSULB University Library Digital Depository, Virtual Oral/Aural History Archive.
Hal Lynch, interview with the author, January 26, 2015.
Jon Regnier, interview with the author, August 1, 2014; October 31, 2014.
Brian Trimble, interview with the author, January 6, 2015.

6. Seventeen Years with Stephen Horn

Dee Abrahamse, interview with the author, August 4, 2014.
David Bernstein, interview with the author, August 29, 2014.
Stephen Horn, interview by Ann Andriesse, August 7, 1991, transcript, provided by the Horn family.
Steve Horn Jr., interview with the author, December 10, 2014.
Mark Mayuga, interview with the author, October 18, 2014.
Perry Moore, interview with the author, January 14, 2015.
Ron Schmidt, interview with the author, January 31, 2015.
Rosemary Taylor Schmidt, interview with the author, January 20, 2015.
Danny Tarkanian, interview with the author, March 13, 2015.

7. Campus Life Is a-Changin'

Dee Abrahamse, interview with the author, August 4, 2014.
C.J. Klug, interview with the author, February 23, 2015.
Gary Little, interview with the author, March 17, 2015.
Dana Rohrabacher, interview with the author, March 21, 2015.
Rosemary Taylor Schmidt, interview with the author, January 20 and 31, 2015.
Bill Spater, interview with the author, January 24, 2015.

Lois Swanson, interview by Rosemary Taylor Schmidt, April 8, 1978, audio file, CSULB Archives.
Bill Tilney, interview with the author, January 20, 2015.

8. The Tarkanian Years and the Gold Mine Gym

David Bernstein, interview with the author, August 29, 2014.
Gary Little, interview with the author, July 10, 2014.
Glenn McDonald, interview with the author, September 15, 2014.
Danny Tarkanian, interview with the author, March 13, 2015.

9. Play Days

Joan Bonvicini, interview with the author, September 5, 2014.
Dorothy Deatherage, interview by Kaye Briegel, February 25, 1981, CSULB University Library Digital Repository, Virtual Oral/Aural History Archive.
Dorothy Deatherage, interview with the author, September 5, 2014.
Gary Little, interview with the author, July 10, 2014.
John McConnell, interview with the author, September 15, 2014.
Perry Moore, interview with the author, March 14, 2015.
Pat Reid, interviewer unknown, November 19, 1979.
Penny Toler, interview with the author, September 8, 2014.

10. That Championship Season

Brian Gimmillaro, interview with the author, July 18, 2014.
Debbie Green, interview with the author, October 4, 2014.
Misty May, interview with the author, August 15, 2014.
Melissa Ohta, interview with the author, November 29, 2014.
Penny Toler, interview with the author, September 8, 2014.

11. Robert Maxson

Dee Abrahamse, interview with the author, August 4, 2014.
Dianne Asis, interview with the author, December 21, 2014.

Valerie Bordeaux, interview with the author, August 12, 2014.
Scott Charmack, interview with the author, January 4, 2015.
Robert Maxson, interview with the author, July 31, 2014.
Doug Robinson, interview with the author, August 21, 2014.

12. The Pyramid

Scott Charmack, interview with the author, January 4 and March 14, 2015.
Don Gibbs, interview with the author, November 13 and 14, 2014.
Andy Jones, interview with the author, November 17, 2014.
Jon Regnier, interview with the author, August 1, 2014; October 31, 2014; November 11, 2014.
Joseph Sopo, interview with the author, November 14, 2014.
Daryl Supernaw, interview with the author, November 14, 2014.

13. Puvungna

Cindi Alvitre, interview with the author, March 26 and 28, 2015.
Jane Close Conoley, interview with the author, March 10, 2015.
Carl Lipo, interview with the author, March 11, 2015.
Ron Loewe, interview with the author, January 8, 2015.
Jon Regnier, interview with the author, August 1, 2014.

14. Football, Greek Housing and Historic Preservation

David Bernstein, interview with the author, August 29, 2014.
Lee Brown, interview with the author, August 14, 2014; February 7, 2015.
Scott Charmack, interview with the author, March 14, 2015.
Jane Close Conoley, interview with the author, March 10, 2015.
Perry Moore, interview with the author, March 14, 2015.
Brett Waterfield, interview with the author, March 20, 2015.
Lauren Weiss, interview with the author, March 20, 2015.

15. The Famous

David Bernstein, interview with the author, August 29, 2014.
Mary Breuer, interview with the author, August 6, 2014.
Steve Martin, speech while receiving honorary doctorate, August 25, 1989, video, CSULB University Library Archive.
Dana Rohrabacher, interview with the author, March 21, 2015.
Stu Rosen, interview with the author, March 26, 2015.
Dave Snow, interview with the author, March 19, 2015.
Lee Vail, interview with the author, December 18, 2014.

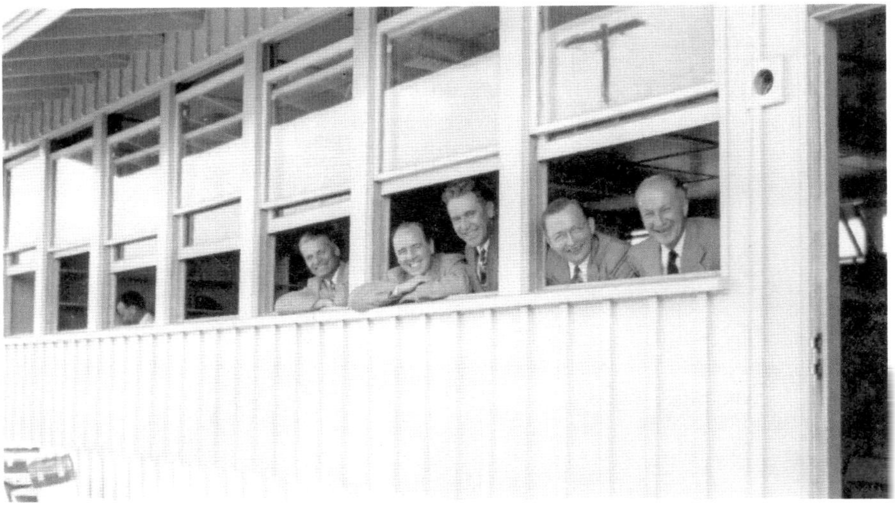

Peekaboo from the library. Original Long Beach State librarian Charles Boorkman is second from right. *Courtesy of the University Archives.*

OTHER SOURCES

Bernstein, David, and Kaye Briegel. "California State University, Long Beach: A Historical Overview." Unpublished. California State University, Long Beach, 1989.

Coleman, Ray. *The Carpenters: The Untold Story, an Authorized Biography*. New York: HarperCollins, 1994.

Grobaty, Tim. *Growing Up in Long Beach: Boomer Memories from Autoettes to Los Altos Drive-In*. Charleston, SC: The History Press, 2013.

Guardabascio, Mike. *Football in Long Beach*. Charleston, SC: The History Press, 2012.

Hillburg, Bill, and Tim Grobaty. *Long Beach: The City and Its People*. Carlsbad, CA: Heritage Media Corp, 2000.

May Treanor, Misty, and Jill Lieber Steeg. *Misty: Digging Deep in Volleyball and Life*. New York: Scribner, 2010.

Russell, Karl A., Jr. *The First Decade of Long Beach State College, 1949–1959*. Long Beach, CA: Long Beach State College, 1960.

Volland, Jennifer M., and Cara Mullio. *Edward A. Killingsworth: An Architect's Life*. Santa Monica, CA: Hennesey and Ingalls, 2013.

Index

About the Author

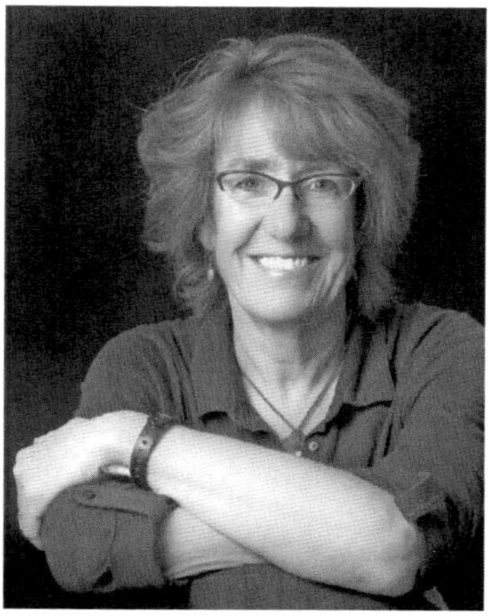

Barbara Kingsley-Wilson has been a full-time lecturer and the adviser for the *49er* since 2004. She was a journalist for twenty years, covering courts, crime, education and sports for the *Orange County Register*, the *Cleveland Plain Dealer* and the *Rochester Times-Union*. She also wrote sports pieces for *USA Today* and worked as an intern with the Associated Press in Tel Aviv, Israel. She graduated from Ohio University with a bachelor's degree in journalism and later earned her master's degree and taught news writing as a fellow in the Kiplinger Mid-Career Reporting Program at Ohio State University. She spent one summer in Amman, Jordan, as part of a United States grant to study women and sports. She has won awards from the Associated Press and the Orange County Press Club and contributed articles to an *O.C. Register* project that won the Pulitzer Prize. She lives with her family in Long Beach.

Visit us at
www.historypress.net

This title is also available as an e-book